conte

2nd edition February 1998
1st edition February 1996

© The Automobile Association 1998

The Automobile Association retains the copyright in the original edition © 1996 and in all subsequent editions, reprints and amendments to editions listed above.

Published by AA Publishing (a trading name of Automobile Association Developments Limited, whose registered office is Norfolk House, Priestley Road, Basingstoke, Hampshire RG24 9NY. Registered number 1878835).

Mapping produced by the Cartographic Department of The Automobile Association. This atlas has been compiled and produced from the Automaps database utilising electronic and computer technology.

ISBN 0 7495 1757 3

A CIP catalogue for this book is available from The British Library.

Printed in Great Britain by BPC Waterlow Ltd, Dunstable.

The contents of this atlas are believed to be correct at the time of printing. Nevertheless, the publishers cannot be held responsible for any errors or omissions, or for changes in the details given. They would welcome information to help keep this atlas up to date; please write to the Cartographic Editor, Publishing Division, The Automobile Association, Norfolk House, Priestley Road, Basingstoke, Hampshire RG24 9NY.

map pages

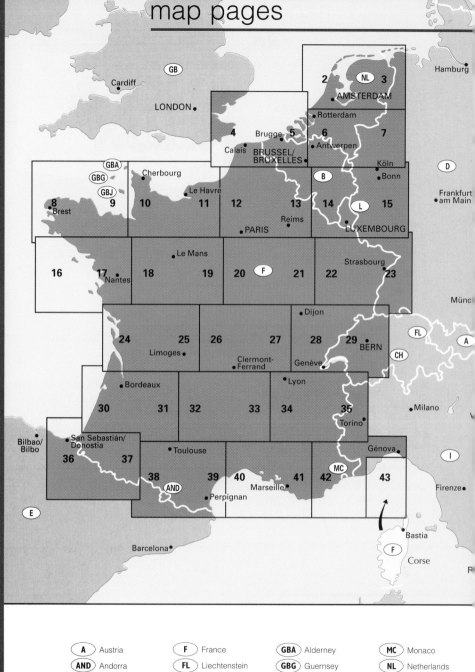

ii

A	Austria	F	France	GBA	Alderney	MC	Monaco
AND	Andorra	FL	Liechtenstein	GBG	Guernsey	NL	Netherlands
B	Belgium	GB	United Kingdom of Great Britain and Northern Ireland	GBJ	Jersey	RSM	San Marino
CH	Switzerland			I	Italy		
D	Germany			L	Luxembourg		
E	Spain						

map symbols

Toll motorways

A55 / **E55**	Dual carriageway with road numbers
	Single carriageway
Interchange	Interchange
Restricted interchange	Restricted interchange
S	Service area
	Under construction

Non-toll motorways

A55 / **E55**	Dual carriageway with road numbers
	Single carriageway
	Interchange
	Restricted interchange
S	Service area
	Under construction

National roads

SS45	Dual carriageway with road number
	Single carriageway

Regional roads

SS45	Dual carriageway with road number
	Single carriageway

Local roads

SS453	Dual carriageway with road number
	Single carriageway
D28	Minor road with road number

 38   Page overlap and number

Symbols

(E55) E55	European international network numbers
	Motorway in tunnel
	Road in tunnel
	Road under construction
☖	Toll point
▼ 24 ▼	Distances in kilometres
>>	Gradient 14% and over
>	Gradient 6%-13%
10-6 ▼ Furkapass	Mountain pass with closure period
2431 3970 ▲ EIGER	Spot height (metres)
⬢	Ferry route (all year)
⬢	Hovercraft (all year)
⊕	Airport (International)
+++++++	Car transporter (rail)
	Mountain railway
· ⚑	Motor racing circuit
☀ ☀	Viewpoint (180° or 360°)
	Urban area
▭	Town location
	Canal
	Wooded area

Boundaries

	International
+ · + · + · + ·	National
– – – –	Unrecognised international
⊗	Restricted frontier crossing

scale

1:1 000 000   10 kilometres : 1 centimetre

16 miles : 1 inch

iii

GBM

■ DUBLIN

Leeds
Liverpool
Manchester
Hull
A55
A5
GB
Birmingham
Norwich
M54
Oxford
Cardiff
LONDON
Southampton
Plymouth
Portsmouth
Dover
Calais

GBA
GBG
GBJ

Cherbourg
Le Havre
Caen
Rouen
Reims
PARIS
Brest
St Malo
Rennes
Le Mans
Orléans
Nantes
Tours
Bourges
Dijon
Limoges
Clermont-Ferrand
Lyon
Bordeaux
F
Grenoble
Bilbao/Bilbo
San Sebastián/Donostia
Pau
Toulouse
Nîmes
Nice
Pamplona/Iruñea
Montpellier
Marseille
Andorra la Vella
AND
Perpignan
Zaragoza
E
Barcelona

AMSTERDAM
Den Haag
Rotterdam
NL
Arnhem
Bielefeld
Vlissingen
Oostende
Brugge
Antwerpen
Essen
BRUSSEL/BRUXELLES
B
Köln
Lille
Liège
Bonn
Charleroi
Amiens
L
LUXEMBOURG
Metz
Nancy
Strasbourg
Basel
BERN
CH
Genève
Torino
Milano
MC
Corse
Ajaccio
Bonifacio

Brugge - Rotterdam = 183 km

183

Afstandstabel / distance chart — steden (diagonaal):

Amsterdam (NL) · Andorra la Vella (AND) · Antwerpen (B) · Arnhem (NL) · Barcelona (E) · Bern (CH) · Bonn (D) · Bordeaux (F) · Brest (F) · Brugge (B) · Brussel/Bruxelles (B) · Calais (F) · Cherbourg (F) · Clermont-Ferrand (F) · Den Haag (NL) · Dijon (F) · Genève (CH) · Groningen (NL) · Le Havre (F) · Le Mans (F) · Liège (B) · Limoges (F) · Luxembourg (L) · Lyon (F) · Marseille (F) · Milano (I) · Nantes (F) · Nice (F) · Oostende (B) · Orléans (F) · Paris (F) · Perpignan (F) · Reims (F) · Rotterdam (NL) · San Sebastián/Donostia (E) · St-Malo (F) · Strasbourg (F) · Toulouse (F) · Tours (F) · Vlissingen (NL)

Triangular distance chart (distances in km, each row lists the distance to every preceding city):

```
Andorra la Vella       1524
Antwerpen              159  1362
Arnhem                 105  1531 166
Barcelona              1600 192  1443 1554
Bern                   841  967  714  745  973
Bonn                   289  1389 226  193  1395 570
Bordeaux               1098 430  936  1105 635  894  1094
Brest                  1114 1051 1122 1111 1576 861  308  625
Brugge                 265  1311 103  272  1438 781  332  901  625
Brussel/Bruxelles      210  1322 50   217  1402 674  231  896  913  97
Calais                 366  1309 205  374  1436 811  432  883  913  110  198
Cherbourg              770  1077 609  778  1300 931  822  651  400  730  549  470
Clermont-Ferrand       942  601  780  949  658  531  825  363  849  883  625  727
Den Haag               64   1497 132  124  1576 861  308  1071 1067 214  198  549  727
Dijon                  738  858  581  692  248  864  533  772  871  577  740  729  183  339  915
Genève                 1004 803  763  908  164  733  356  1253 1270 759  574  625  214  743
Groningen              183  1679 314  172  1726 908  638  1218 465  420  679  925
Le Havre               586  1043 424  593  1218 775  593  638  617  364  285  204  568  502
Le Mans                718  866  556  725  714  440  405  714  440  505  516  279  686  298
Liège                  243  1351 119  197  1357 628  139  958  974  197  96   298  710  695
Limoges                911  493  750  919  717  676  908  221  598  698  710  567  177  884
Luxembourg             410  1184 253  364  1190 461  206  950  966  320  212  414  733  620
Lyon                   932  646  775  886  652  317  727  1061 1023 771  734  768  831  179
Marseille              1266 515  1220 522  639  1061 649  1270 1413 1105 1069 1102 485  242
Milano                 1082 992  955  986  998  350  811  1126 1413 1022 914  1105 631  1101
Nantes                 899  756  738  907  979  681  607  330  293  686  698  734  313  179
Nice                   1396 675  1264 1300 681  607  1125 1428 809  1259 1223 1257 640  357
Oostende               282  1328 121  290  1456 799  349  902  795  25   114  95   534  293
Orléans                648  886  487  656  952  645  460  548  601  435  447  433  430  357
Paris                  509  1010 347  516  1190 564  505  584  601  234  293  307  428  293
Perpignan              1395 167  1239 1350 208  769  1191 449  1069 1234 1198 1232 1094 451
Reims                  485  1146 332  492  1160 535  437  720  736  281  275  278  503  564
Rotterdam              92   1465 100  119  1544 855  303  1335 1055 151  307  711  883  307
San Sebastián/Donostia 1338 451  1177 1346 569  1200 1036 186  383  865  858  609  1006 1311
St-Malo                819  943  557  826  1166 944  517  871  517  597  673  518  188  671
Strasbourg             628  1156 472  524  1163 239  331  1063 1080 539  622  845  605  333
Toulouse               1338 188  1177 1346 409  857  1279 244  865  1125 1137 1123 891  408
Tours                  750  776  798  1000 669  747  350  470  537  549  535  359  723  147
Vlissingen             209  1353 88   216  1531 802  309  927  944  43   151  307  711  592
```

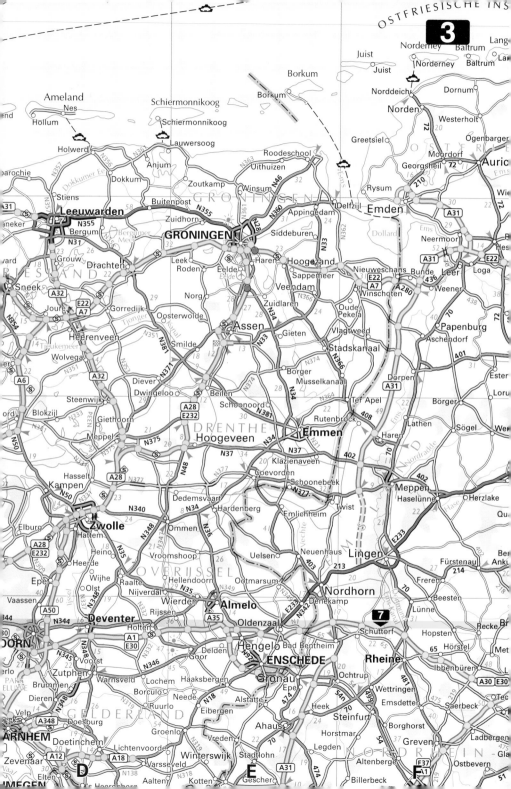

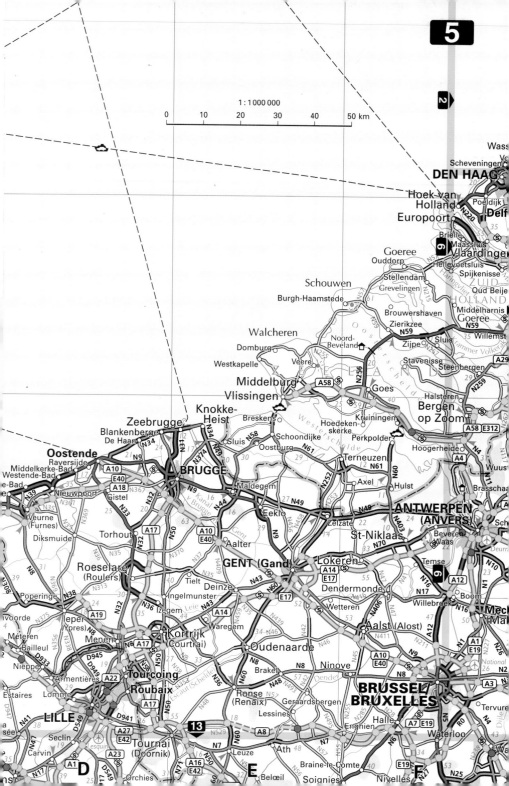

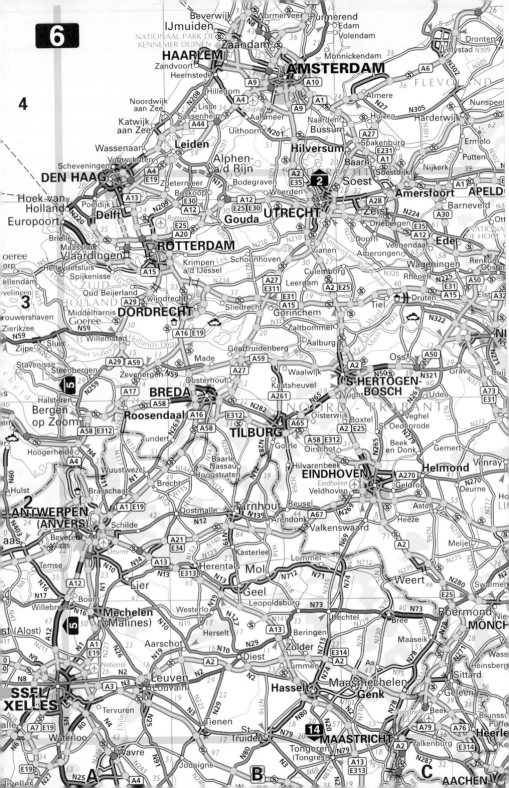

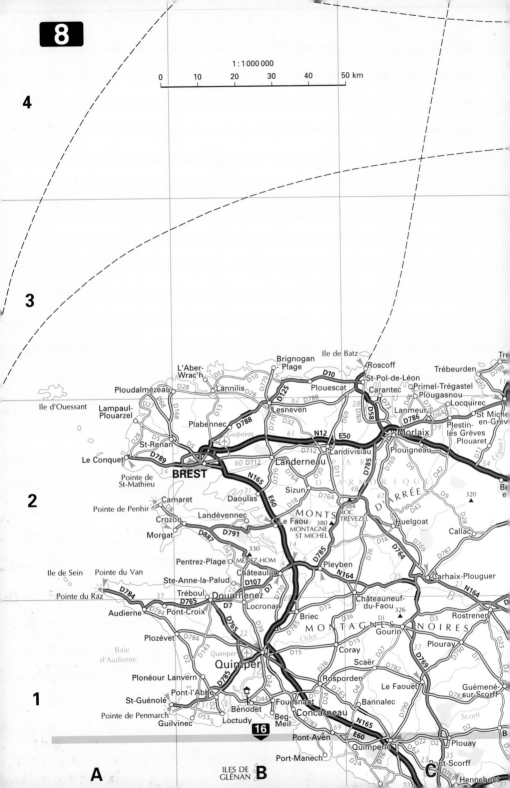

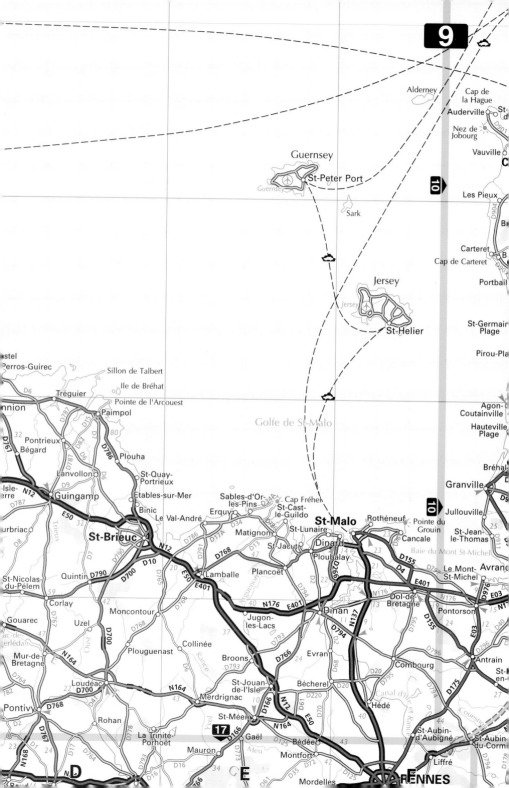

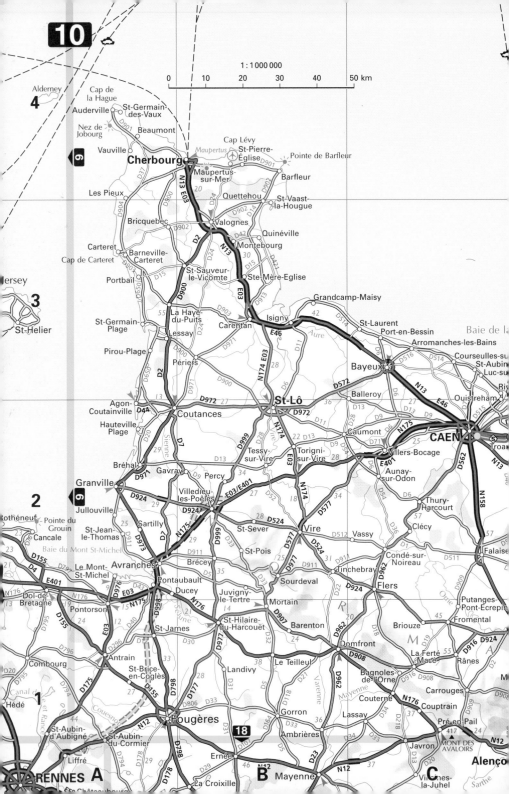

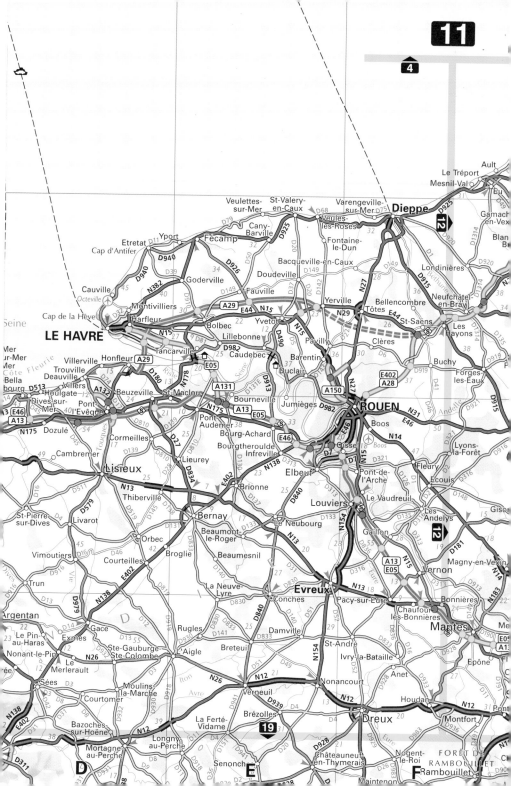

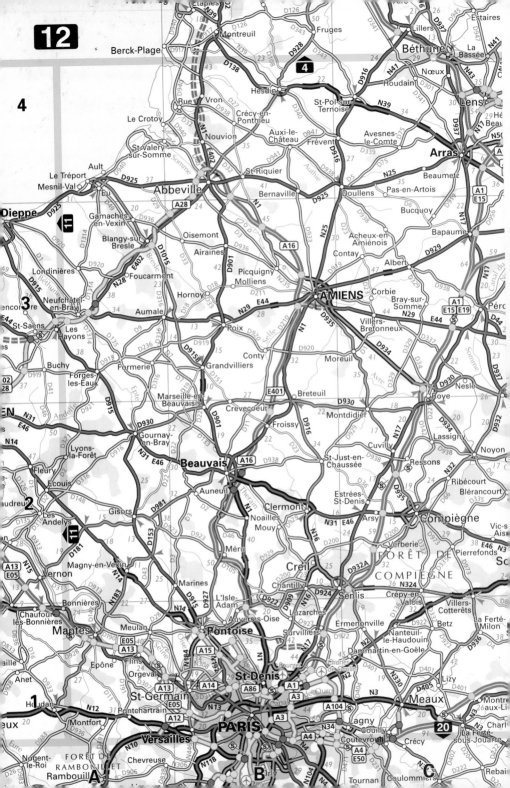

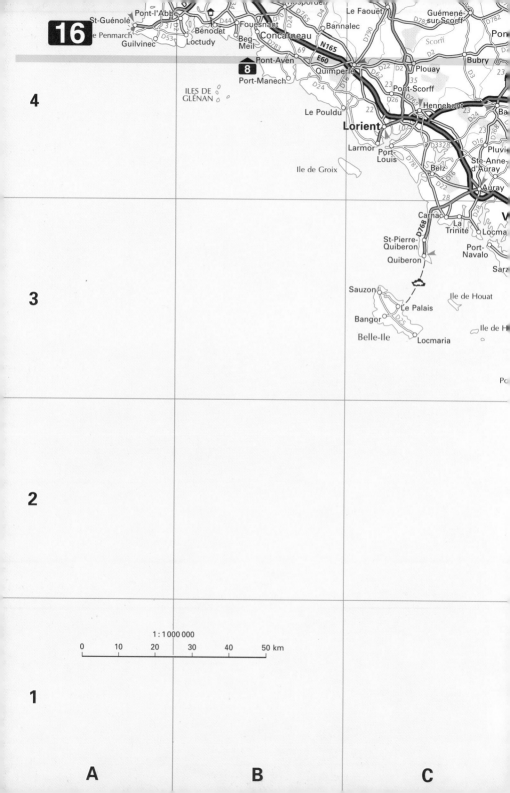

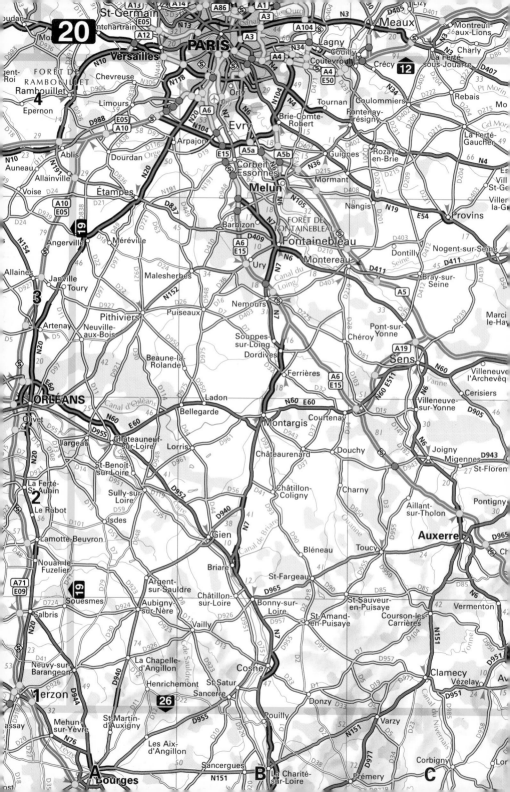

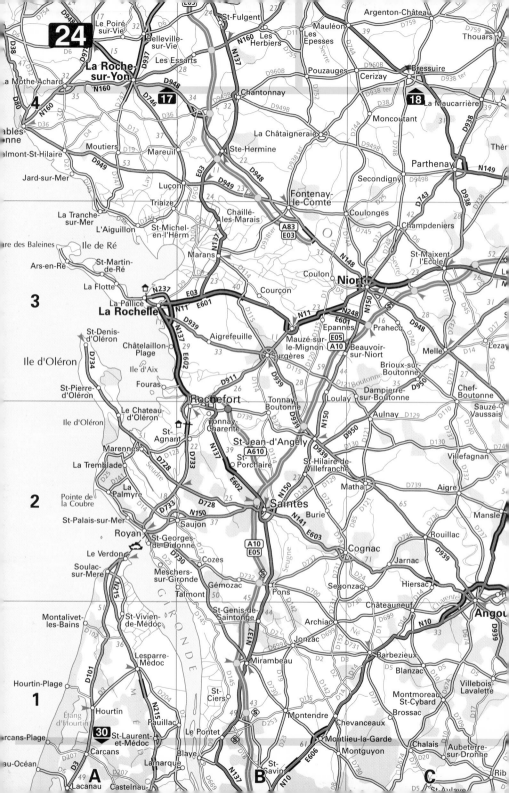

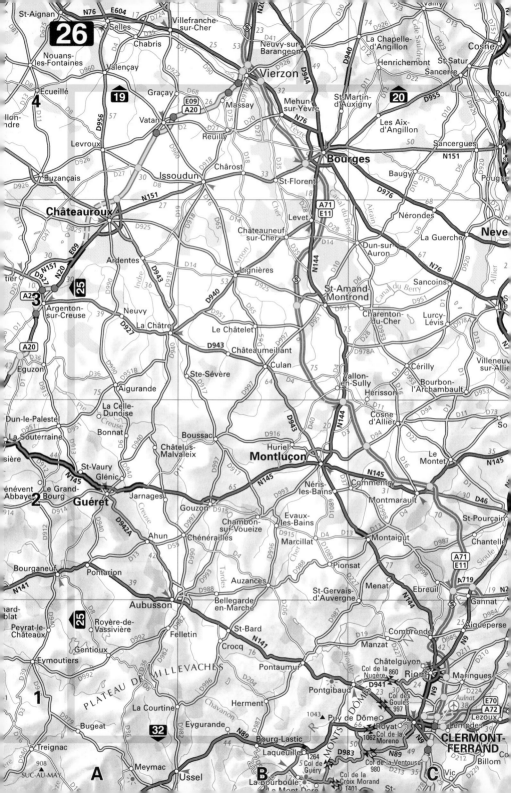

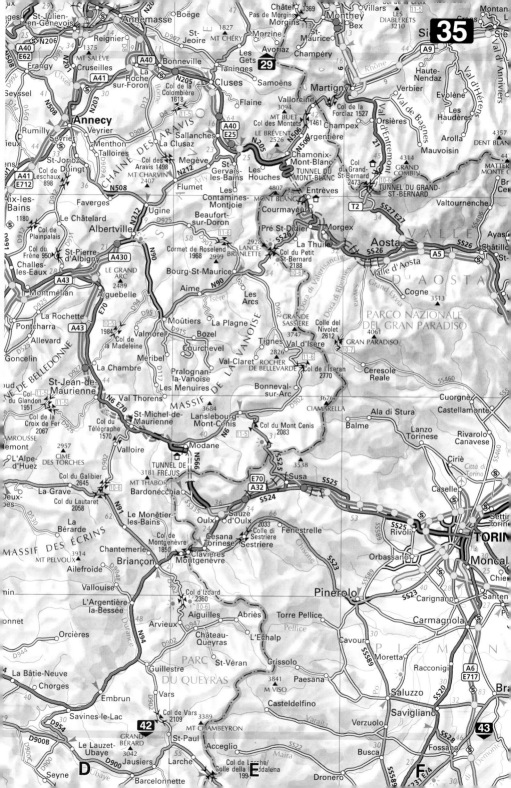

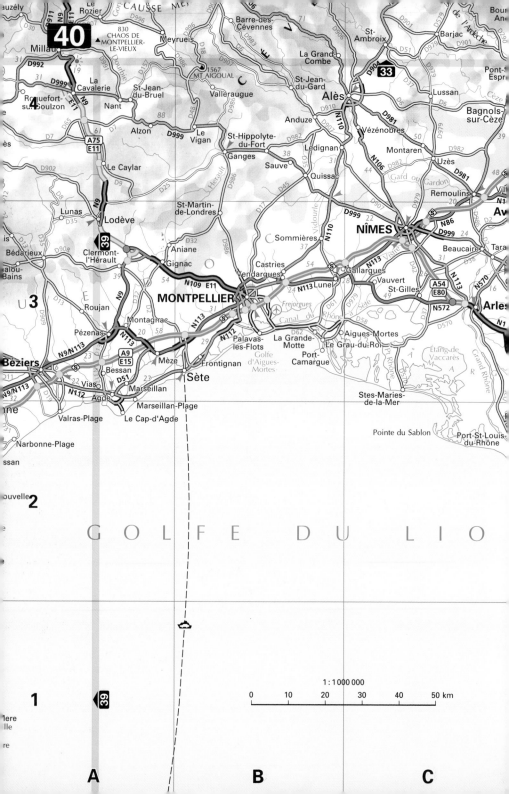

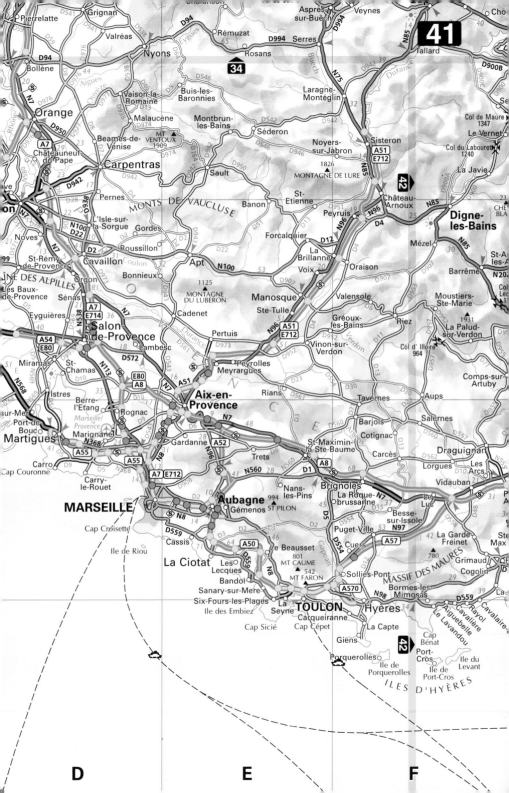

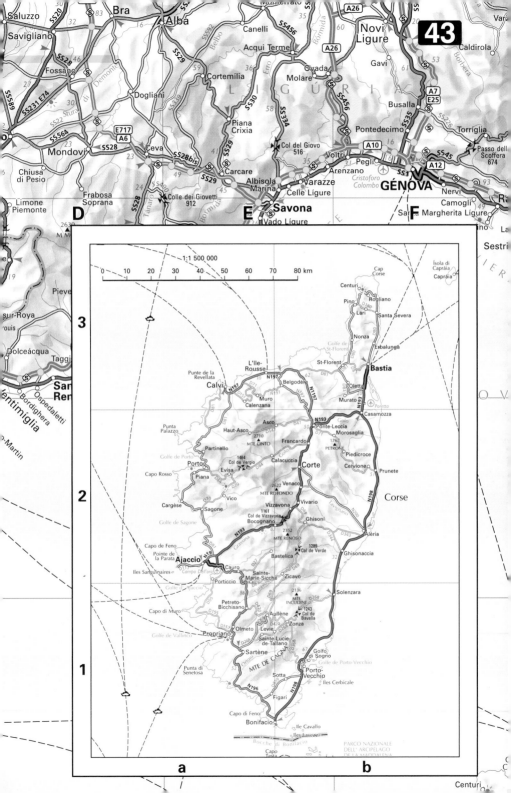

A

Ahaus D	7	E3	Aizenay F	17	E1	Alsasua E	36	A3
Ahlen D	7	F2	Ajaccio F	43	a2	Alsenz D	15	E1
Ahrweiler D	15	E3	Ala di Stura I	35	F2	Alstätte D	7	E3
Ahun F	26	A2	Alba I	43	D4	Altena D	7	F1
Aigle CH	29	D1	Alban F	39	E4	Altenahr D	15	D3
Aachen D	14	C4	Aignay-le-Duc F	21	E1	Albens F	35	D4	Altenberge D	7	F3
Aalburg NL	6	B3	Aigre F	24	C2	Albert F	12	C3	Altenglan D	15	E1
Aalsmeer NL	2	B2	Aigrefeuille F	24	B3	Albertville F	35	D3	Altenhundem D	15	F4
Aalst (Alost) B	5	F1	Aigrefeuille-sur-Maine F	17	E2	Albi F	39	D4	Altenkirchen D	15	F4
Aalten NL	7	E3	Aiguebelle F	42	A1	Albisola Marina I	43	E4	Altensteig D	23	F2
Aalter B	5	E2	Aiguebelle F	35	D3	Aldeburgh GB	4	C4	Altkirch F	29	E4
Aarau CH	29	F3	Aigueperse F	26	C1	Aldenhoven D	15	D4	Alvignac F	32	A3
Aarberg CH	29	E3	Aigues-Mortes F	40	B3	Alençon F	18	C4	Alzey D	15	F1
Aarburg CH	29	F3	Aiguilles F	35	E1	Aléria F	43	b2	Alzon F	40	A4
Aarschot B	6	B1	Aiguillon F	31	D2	Alés F	40	C4	Alzonne F	39	D3
Abbeville F	12	B4	Aigurande F	26	A3	Alf D	15	E2	Amance F	22	B1
Ablis F	19	F4	Ailefroide F	35	D2	Alfaro E	36	A1	Amancey F	28	C3
Abondance F	29	D1	Aillant-sur-Tholon F	20	C2	Alkmaar NL	2	B2	Amay B	14	B4
Abreschviller F	23	D3	Aime F	35	E3	Allaines F	19	F3	Ambarès F	30	C4
Abriès F	35	E1	Ainhoa F	36	B3	Allainville F	19	F4	Ambazac F	25	E2
Acceglio I	42	C4	Ainsa E	37	E1	Allanche F	33	D3	Ambérieu-en-Bugey F	34	C4
Accous F	37	D2	Airaines F	12	B3	Allemont F	34	C2	Ambert F	33	E4
Achern D	23	E3	Aire F	4	C1	Allevard F	35	D3	Amboise F	19	D2
Acheux-en-Amiénois F	12	C3	Aire-sur-l'Adour F	37	E4	Allonnes F	18	C2	Ambrières F	10	B1
Acqui Terme I	43	E4	Airvault F	24	C4	Allos F	42	B4	Amélie-les-Bains F	39	D1
Adelboden CH	29	E1	Aisey-sur-Seine F	21	E1	Almelo NL	3	E1	Amerongen NL	6	C3
Adenau D	15	D3	Aïssey F	29	D3	Almere NL	2	C2	Amersfoort NL	6	C4
Agay F	42	B2	Aisy-sur-Armançon F	21	D1	Alost (Aalst) B	5	F1	Amiens F	12	B3
Agde F	40	A3	Aix-en-Othe F	21	D3	Alp E	38	C1	Amou F	37	D4
Agen F	31	D2	Aix-en-Provence F	41	E2	Alpen D	7	D2	Amphion F	29	D1
Agon-Coutainville F	10	A2	Aix-les-Bains F	34	C3	Alphen-aan den Rijn NL	2	B1	Amplepuis F	27	E1
Agoncillo E	36	A2	Aixe-sur-Vienne F	25	E1	Alpirsbach D	23	F2	Ampuis F	34	B3

Amsterdam NL...... 2 B2
Ancenis F...... 17 F2
Ancerville F...... 21 F3
Ancy-le-Franc F...... 21 D2
Andelot F...... 21 F2
Andenne B...... 14 B4
Andernach D...... 15 E3
Andernos-les-Bains F...... 30 B3
Andijk NL...... 2 C3
Andolsheim F...... 23 D2
Andorra la Vella AND...... 38 B1
Andrézieux-Bouthéon F.... 33 F3
Anduze F...... 40 B4
Anet F...... 11 F1
Angers F...... 18 B2
Angerville F...... 20 A3
Anglet F...... 36 C4
Anglure F...... 21 D3
Angoulême F...... 24 C2
Aniane F...... 40 A3
Aniche F...... 13 D4
Anjum NL...... 3 D4
Anna Paulowna NL...... 2 B3
Annecy F...... 35 D4
Annemasse F...... 28 C1
Annonay F...... 34 A3
Annot F...... 42 B3
Annweiler D...... 23 E4
Anse F...... 34 B4
Anseremme B...... 14 A3
Anthéor F...... 42 B2
Antibes F...... 42 C2
Antraigues F...... 33 F2
Antrain F...... 10 A1
Antwerpen (Anvers) B...... 6 A2
Anvers (Antwerpen) B...... 6 A2
Aoiz E...... 36 B2
Aosta I...... 35 F3
Apeldoorn NL...... 7 D4
Appelhülsen D...... 7 F3
Appenweier D...... 23 E2
Appingedam NL...... 3 E3
Apt F...... 41 E3
Aramits F...... 37 D3
Aranaz/Echarri E...... 36 A3
Arbois F...... 28 B3
Arc-en-Barrois F...... 21 F2
Arcachon F...... 30 B3
Arcen NL...... 7 D2
Arches F...... 22 C2
Archiac F...... 24 B1
Arcis-sur-Aube F...... 21 D3
Ardentes F...... 26 A3
Ardres F...... 4 C2
Arendonk B...... 6 B2
Arenzano I...... 43 E4
Arès F...... 30 B4
Argancy F...... 22 C4
Argelès-Gazost F...... 37 E2
Argelès-Plage F...... 39 E2
Argelès-sur-Mer F...... 39 E1
Argent-sur-Sauldre F...... 20 A2
Argentan F...... 10 C1
Argentat F...... 32 B3
Argentière F...... 35 E4
Argenton-Château F... 18 B1
Argenton-sur-Creuse F... 25 F3
Argentré F...... 18 B4
Arguedas E...... 36 B1
Arguis E...... 37 D1
Arinthod F...... 28 B2
Arlanc F...... 33 E3
Arles F...... 40 C3
Arles-sur-Tech F...... 39 D1
Arlon B...... 14 B2
Armentières F...... 5 D1
Arnage F...... 18 C3
Arnay-le-Duc F...... 27 F3
Arnedo E...... 36 A1
Arnhem NL...... 7 D3
Arolla CH...... 35 F4
Arpajon F...... 20 A4
Arracourt F...... 22 C3
Arras F...... 12 C4

Arreau F...... 37 E2
Arrens-Marsous F...... 37 D2
Arromanches-les-Bains F.. 10 C3
Ars-en-Ré F...... 24 A3
Ars-sur-Moselle F...... 22 B4
Arsy F...... 12 C2
Artemare F...... 34 C4
Artenay F...... 19 F3
Arties E...... 38 A2
Artix F...... 37 D3
Arudy F...... 37 D2
Arvieux F...... 35 E1
Arzacq-Arraziguet F...... 37 D3
As B...... 6 C1
Ascain F...... 36 B3
Ascheberg D...... 7 F2
Aschendorf D...... 3 F3
Asco F...... 43 b2
Asfeld F...... 13 E2
Ashford GB...... 4 A3
Aspet F...... 38 A3
Aspres-sur-Buëch F...... 34 C1
Assen NL...... 3 E3
Assmannshausen D...... 15 F2
Astaffort F...... 31 D2
Asten NL...... 6 C2
Ath B...... 13 E4
Attendorn D...... 7 F1
Attigny F...... 13 F2
Aubagne F...... 41 E2
Aubange B...... 14 B2
Aubenas F...... 33 F2
Auberive F...... 21 F1
Aubeterre-sur-Dronne F... 31 D4
Aubigny-sur-Nere F...... 20 A1
Auboué F...... 22 B4
Aubusson F...... 26 A1
Auch F...... 38 A4
Audenge F...... 30 B3
Auderville F...... 10 A4
Audeux F...... 28 C3
Audierne F...... 8 A1
Audincourt F...... 29 D4
Audressein F...... 38 B2
Audun-le-Roman F...... 14 B1
Aullène F...... 43 a1
Aulnay F...... 24 C2
Ault F...... 12 A4
Aulus-les-Bains F...... 38 B2
Aumale F...... 12 A3
Aumetz F...... 14 C1
Aumont-Aubrac F...... 33 D2
Aunay-sur-Odon F...... 10 C2
Auneau F...... 19 F4
Auneuil F...... 12 B2
Aups F...... 42 A3
Auray F...... 16 C4
Aurich D...... 3 F4
Aurignac F...... 38 B3
Aurillac F...... 32 C3
Auron F...... 42 B4
Auterive F...... 38 C3
Authon-du-Perche F...... 19 D3
Autun F...... 27 E3
Auvers-s-Oise F...... 12 B1
Auvillers-les-Forges F...... 13 E2
Auxerre F...... 20 C2
Auxi-le-Château F...... 12 B4
Auxonne F...... 28 B3
Auzances F...... 26 B2
Auzon F...... 33 D3
Availles-Limouzine F...... 25 D2
Avallon F...... 21 D1
Avenches CH...... 29 E2
Avesnes-le-Comte F...... 12 C4
Avesnes-sur-Helpe F...... 13 E3
Avignon F...... 41 D3
Avoriaz F...... 29 D1
Avranches F...... 10 A2
Ax-les-Thermes F...... 38 C2
Axat F...... 39 D2
Axel NL...... 5 F2
Ay F...... 13 E1
Ayerbe E...... 36 C1

Azay-le-Rideau F...... 18 C2
Azpeitia E...... 36 A3

B

Baarle Nassau NL...... 6 B2
Baarn NL...... 2 C1
Baccarat F...... 22 C2
Bacharach D...... 15 F2
Bacqueville-en-Caux F.... 11 F3
Bad Bentheim D...... 7 E4
Bad Bergzabern D...... 23 E4
Bad Bertrich D...... 15 D2
Bad Breisig D...... 15 E3
Bad Dürkheim D...... 15 F1
Bad Dürrheim D...... 23 F1
Bad Ems D...... 15 F3
Bad Godesberg D...... 15 E4
Bad Herrenalb D...... 23 F3
Bad Honnef D...... 15 E3
Bad Hönnigen D...... 15 E3
Bad Kreuznach D...... 15 F2
Bad Krozingen D...... 23 E1
Bad Liebenzell D...... 23 F3
Bad Marienberg D...... 15 F3
Bad Münster
  Ebernburg D...... 15 F2
Bad Münstereifel D...... 15 D3
Bad Neuenahr D...... 15 E3
Bad Peterstal D...... 23 F2
Bad Rippoldsau D...... 23 F2
Bad Säckingen D...... 29 F4
Bad Schönborn D...... 23 F3
Bad Schwalbach D...... 15 F2
Baden-Baden D...... 23 F3
Badenweiler D...... 29 F4
Badonviller F...... 22 C3
Bagà E...... 38 C1
Bagnères-de-Bigorre F.... 37 E2
Bagnères-de-Luchon F... 37 F1
Bagnoles-de-l'Orne F...... 10 C1
Bagnols-en-Forêt F...... 42 B2
Bagnols-les-Bains F...... 33 E2
Bagnols-sur-Cèze F...... 40 C4
Baiersbronn D...... 23 F2
Baigneux-les-Juifs F...... 21 E1
Bailleul F...... 5 D1
Bain-de-Bretagne F...... 17 E3
Bains-les-Bains F...... 22 B2
Bais F...... 18 B4
Baix F...... 34 A2
Baixas F...... 39 E2
Balbigny F...... 33 F4
Balleroy F...... 10 C3
Ballon F...... 18 C3
Balme I...... 35 F2
Balneario de Panticosa E... 37 D2
Balsthal CH...... 29 F3
Baltrum D...... 3 F4
Bandol F...... 41 E2
Bangor F...... 16 C3
Bannalec F...... 8 C1
Bannon F...... 41 E3
Banyuls-sur-Mer F...... 39 E1
Bapaume F...... 12 C3
Bar-le-Duc F...... 21 F3
Bar-sur-Aube F...... 21 E2
Bar-sur-Seine F...... 21 E2
Baraqueville F...... 32 B1
Barbaste F...... 31 D2
Barbezieux F...... 24 C1
Barbotan-les-Thermes F... 30 C2
Barcelonnette F...... 42 B4
Bardonécchia I...... 35 E2
Barentin F...... 11 E3
Barenton F...... 10 B1
Barfleur F...... 10 B4
Barjac F...... 33 F1
Barjols F...... 41 F2

Barneveld NL...... 6 C3
Barneville-Carteret F...... 10 A3
Barr F...... 23 D2
Barre-des-Cévennes F..... 33 D1
Barrême F...... 42 A3
Basel CH...... 29 F4
Basildon GB...... 4 A4
Bastelica F...... 43 a2
Bastia F...... 43 b3
Bastogne B...... 14 B2
Battice B...... 14 C4
Batz-sur-Mer F...... 17 D3
Baud F...... 16 C4
Baugé F...... 18 C2
Baugy F...... 26 C4
Baume-les-Dames F...... 29 D3
Baumholder D...... 15 E1
Bavay F...... 13 E3
Bawdsey GB...... 4 B4
Bayeux F...... 10 C3
Bayon F...... 22 C3
Bayonne F...... 36 C4
Bazas F...... 30 C3
Bazoches-sur-Hoëne F.... 11 D1
Beames-de-Venise F...... 41 D4
Beaucaire F...... 40 C3
Beaufort-en-Vallée F...... 18 B2
Beaufort-sur-Doron F.... 35 E3
Beaugency F...... 19 E2
Beaulieu-sur-Dordogne F... 32 B3
Beaulieu-sur-Mer F...... 42 C2
Beaumesnil F...... 11 E2
Beaumetz F...... 12 C4
Beaumont F...... 31 E3
Beaumont F...... 10 A4
Beaumont B...... 14 A3
Beaumont-de-Lomagne F.. 31 E1
Beaumont-le-Roger F...... 11 E2
Beaumont-sur-Sarthe F... 18 C4
Beaune F...... 28 A3
Beaune-la-Rolande F...... 20 B3
Beaupréau F...... 18 A2
Beauraing B...... 14 A3
Beaurepaire F...... 34 B3
Beaurepaire-en-Bresse F.. 28 B2
Beauvais F...... 12 B2
Beauvallon F...... 42 B2
Beauvezer F...... 42 B4
Beauvoir-sur-Mer F...... 17 D2
Beauvoir-sur-Niort F...... 24 B3
Bécherel F...... 9 F1
Beckum D...... 7 F2
Bédarieux F...... 39 F3
Bédée F...... 17 E4
Bedous F...... 37 D2
Beek NL...... 6 C1
Beek en Donk NL...... 6 C2
Beesten D...... 3 F1
Beg-Meil F...... 8 B1
Bégard F...... 9 D2
Beilen NL...... 3 E3
Bélâbre F...... 25 E3
Belcaire F...... 38 C2
Belfort F...... 29 D4
Belgodère F...... 43 b3
Belin-Béliet F...... 30 B3
Bellac F...... 25 E2
Belle-Isle-en-Terre F...... 8 C2
Bellegarde F...... 20 B2
Bellegarde-en-Marche F... 26 B2
Bellegarde-sur-
  Valserine F...... 28 B1
Bellême F...... 19 D4
Bellencombre F...... 11 F3
Belleville F...... 27 F1
Belleville-sur-Vie F...... 17 E1
Belley F...... 34 C4
Bellver de Cerdanya E...... 38 C1
Belmont-sur-Rance F...... 39 E4
Beloeil B...... 13 E4
Belvès F...... 31 E3
Belz F...... 16 C4
Benasque E...... 37 F1
Bénévent l'Abbaye F...... 25 F2

46

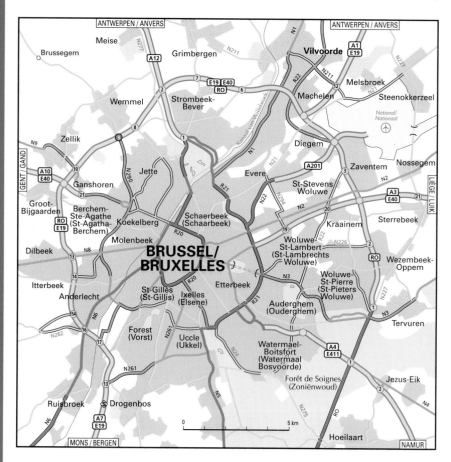

Benfeld F	23	E2	Beuil F	42	C3	Blâmont F	22	C3	Bonn D	15	E4
Bénodet F	8	B1	Beuzeville F	11	D2	Blangy-sur-Bresle F	12	A3	Bonnat F	26	A2
Bensberg D	15	E4	Beveren-Waas B	5	F2	Blankenberge B	5	D2	Bonndorf D	23	F1
Berck-Plage F	4	B1	Beverwijk NL	2	B2	Blankenheim D	15	D3	Bonnétable F	19	D3
Berg-Neustadt D	7	F1	Bex CH	29	D1	Blanzac F	24	C1	Bonneval F	19	E3
Bergara E	36	A3	Beynat-et-Cazenac F	31	F3	Blaye F	30	C4	Bonneval-sur-Arc F	35	E3
Bergen NL	2	B2	Beynat F	32	B3	Bléneau F	20	B2	Bonneville F	35	D4
Bergen (Mons) B	13	E4	Béziers F	39	F3	Blérancourt F	12	C2	Bonnières F	11	F1
Bergen aan Zee NL	2	B2	Biarritz F	36	B4	Bléré F	19	D2	Bonnieux F	41	D3
Bergen op Zoom NL	6	A2	Bias F	30	A2	Blériot-Plage F	4	B2	Bonny-sur-Loire F	20	B1
Bergerac F	31	E3	Biberach D	23	E2	Bletterans F	28	B2	Boom B	6	A2
Bergheim D	7	D1	Bidache F	36	C4	Blieskastel D	23	D4	Boos F	11	F2
Bergisch Gladbach D	7	E1	Bidart F	36	B4	Bligny-sur-Ouche F	27	F3	Boppard D	15	E3
Bergues F	4	C2	Biddenden GB	4	A3	Blois F	19	E2	Borculo NL	7	D3
Bergum NL	3	D3	Biel/Bienne CH	29	E3	Blokzijl NL	3	D2	Bordeaux F	30	C3
Beringen B	6	B1	Bielsa E	37	E1	Blumberg D	23	F1	Bordères F	37	E2
Bern CH	29	E2	Bienne/Biel CH	29	E3	Bocholt D	7	E3	Bordighera I	43	D3
Bernaville F	12	B4	Bierre-Lès-Semur F	27	F4	Bochum D	7	E2	Borger NL	3	E3
Bernay F	11	E2	Biescas F	37	D1	Bockum-Hovel D	7	F2	Börger D	3	F2
Bernkastel-Kues D	15	D2	Billerbeck D	7	F3	Bocognano F	43	a2	Borghorst D	7	F3
Berre-l'Etang F	41	D2	Billericay GB	4	A4	Bodegraven NL	6	B4	Borgo San Dalmazzo I	42	C4
Bertrix B	14	B2	Billom F	33	D4	Boëge F	28	C1	Borken D	7	E3
Besançon F	28	C3	Binas F	19	E3	Boën F	33	F4	Borkum D	3	E4
Bessan F	40	A3	Binche B	13	E4	Bohain-en-Vermandois F	13	D3	Bormes-les-Mimosas F	42	A1
Besse-en-Chandesse F	33	D4	Bingen D	15	E2	Bolbec F	11	E3	Bort-les-Orgues F	32	C4
Besse-sur-Issole F	41	F2	Binic F	9	D2	Bollène F	41	D4	Boskoop NL	6	B4
Bessines-sur-Gartempe F	25	D2	Birkenfeld D	15	D1	Bologne F	21	F2	Bossost E	37	F1
Betelu E	36	A3	Biscarosse F	30	B3	Bolsward NL	2	C3	Bottrop D	7	E2
Béthune F	4	C2	Biscarosse-Plage F	30	A3	Boltaña E	37	E1	Bouaye F	17	E2
Betz F	12	C1	Bitburg D	15	D2	Boltigen CH	29	E2	Boudry CH	29	D2
Betzdorf D	15	F4	Bitche F	23	D4	Bonifacio F	43	a1	Bouillon B	14	A2
Beul D	15	E4	Blain F	17	E3	Bonlieu F	28	C2	Bouilly F	21	D3

Boulay-Moselle F...... 22 C4
Boulogne F...... 4 B1
Boulogne-sur-Gesse F...... 38 A3
Bouloire F...... 19 D3
Bourbon-Lancy F...... 27 D2
Bourbon-l'Archambault F...... 26 C3
Bourbonne-les-Bains F...... 22 A2
Bourbourg F...... 4 C2
Bourbriac F...... 9 D2
Bourdeaux F...... 34 B1
Bourg F...... 30 C4
Bourg-Achard F...... 11 E2
Bourg-Argental F...... 34 A3
Bourg-de-Péage F...... 34 B2
Bourg-en-Bresse F...... 28 A1
Bourg-Lastic F...... 32 C4
Bourg-Madame F...... 38 C1
Bourg-St-Andéol F...... 33 F1
Bourg-St-Maurice F...... 35 E3
Bourganeuf F...... 25 F2
Bourges F...... 26 B4
Bourgneuf-en-Retz F...... 17 E2
Bourgogne F...... 13 E1
Bourgoin-Jallieu F...... 34 B3
Bourgtheroulde-
Infreville F...... 11 E2
Bourgueil F...... 18 C2
Bourmont F...... 22 A2
Bourneville F...... 11 E3
Boussac F...... 26 B2
Boussens F...... 38 B3
Bouvignes B...... 14 A3
Bouvron F...... 17 E3
Bouxwiller F...... 23 D3
Bouzonville F...... 14 C1
Boxmeer NL...... 6 C2
Boxtel NL...... 6 C2
Bozel F...... 35 E3
Bra I...... 35 F1
Bracieux F...... 19 E2
Bradwell-on-Sea GB...... 4 A4
Braine F...... 13 D2
Braine-le-Comte B...... 13 E4
Braintree GB...... 4 A4
Brakel B...... 5 E1
Brancion F...... 27 F2
Branne F...... 30 C3
Brantôme F...... 31 E4
Brassac F...... 39 E3
Brasschaat B...... 6 A2
Braubach D...... 15 E3
Bray-sur-Seine F...... 20 C3
Bray-sur-Somme F...... 12 C3
Brécey F...... 10 B2
Brecht B...... 6 A2
Breda NL...... 6 B3
Bree B...... 6 C1
Bréhal F...... 10 A2
Breil-sur-Roya F...... 42 C3
Breisach D...... 23 D1
Breskens NL...... 5 E2
Bressuire F...... 18 B1
Brest F...... 8 B2
Bretenoux F...... 32 B3
Breteuil F...... 12 B3
Breteuil F...... 11 E1
Breuil-Cervinia I...... 35 F4
Brézolles F...... 11 E1
Briançon F...... 35 D2
Briare F...... 20 B2
Bricquebec F...... 10 A3
Brie-Comte-Robert F...... 20 B4
Briec F...... 8 B1
Brielle NL...... 6 A3
Brienne-le-Château F...... 21 E3
Brienz CH...... 29 F2
Briey F...... 14 B1
Brig CH...... 29 F1
Brignogan-Plage F...... 8 B3
Brignoles F...... 41 F2
Brignoud F...... 34 C3
Brionne F...... 11 E2
Brioude F...... 33 D3
Brioux-sur-Boutonne F...... 24 C3

Briouze F...... 10 C1
Brissac-Quincé F...... 18 B2
Brive-la-Gaillarde F...... 32 A3
Broadstairs GB...... 4 B3
Brodenbach D...... 15 E3
Broglie F...... 11 D2
Brohl D...... 15 E3
Broons F...... 9 E1
Brossac F...... 24 C1
Broto E...... 37 D1
Brou F...... 19 E3
Brouvelieures F...... 22 C2
Brouwershaven NL...... 5 F3
Bruchsal D...... 23 F4
Brugge B...... 5 E2
Brühl D...... 15 D4
Brûlon F...... 18 C3
Brumath F...... 23 E3
Brummen NL...... 7 D3
Bruniquel F...... 32 A1
Brunssum NL...... 6 C1
Brussel/Bruxelles B...... 5 F1
Bruxelles/Brussel B...... 5 F1
Bruyères F...... 22 C2
Bubry F...... 8 C1
Buchy F...... 11 F3
Bucquoy F...... 12 C3
Bugeat F...... 26 A1
Bühl D...... 23 E3
Buis-les-Baronnies F...... 41 E4
Buitenpost NL...... 3 D3
Bulgnéville F...... 22 B2
Bulle CH...... 29 D2
Bunde D...... 3 F3
Burbach D...... 15 F4
Büren CH...... 29 E3
Burgdorf CH...... 29 F3
Burgh-Haamstede NL...... 5 F3
Burguete E...... 36 C3
Burie F...... 24 B2
Burnham-on-Crouch GB...... 4 A4
Busalla I...... 43 F4
Busca I...... 43 D4
Bussang F...... 22 C1
Bussum NL...... 2 C2
Bütgenbach B...... 14 C3
Buxy F...... 27 F2
Buzançais F...... 25 F4
Buzancy F...... 14 A1

C

Cabourg F...... 11 D2
Cabrerets F...... 32 A2
Cadenet F...... 41 E3
Cadillac F...... 30 C3
Caen F...... 10 C2
Cagnes-sur-Mer F...... 42 C2
Cahors F...... 31 F2
Cajarc F...... 32 A2
Calacuccia F...... 43 a2
Calahorra E...... 36 A1
Calais F...... 4 B2
Caldirola I...... 43 F4
Calenzana F...... 43 a3
Calignac F...... 31 D2
Callac F...... 8 C2
Calvi F...... 43 a3
Calw D...... 23 F3
Camarès F...... 39 E4
Camaret F...... 8 A2
Camberg D...... 15 F3
Cambo-les-Bains F...... 36 C3
Cambrai F...... 13 D3
Cambremer F...... 11 D2
Camogli I...... 43 F3
Campan F...... 37 E2
Campdón E...... 39 D1
Cancale F...... 9 F2
Cancon F...... 31 E2

Candanchú E...... 37 D2
Candé F...... 18 A3
Canelli I...... 43 E4
Canet-Plage F...... 39 E1
Canfranc E...... 37 D2
Cannes F...... 42 B2
Canterbury GB...... 4 A3
Canvey Island GB...... 4 A3
Cany-Barville F...... 11 E3
Cap Ferret F...... 30 B3
Cap Gris Nez F...... 4 B2
Cap-d'Ail F...... 42 C2
Capbreton F...... 30 A1
Capendu F...... 39 D3
Capestang F...... 39 E3
Captieux F...... 30 C2
Caraman F...... 38 C3
Carantec F...... 8 C3
Carbon-Blanc F...... 30 C4
Carbonne F...... 38 B3
Carcans F...... 30 B4
Carcans-Plage F...... 30 B4
Carcare I...... 43 E4
Carcassonne F...... 39 D3
Carcastillo E...... 36 B1
Carcès F...... 41 F2
Carennac F...... 32 A3
Carentan F...... 10 B3
Cargèse F...... 43 a2
Carhaix-Plouguer F...... 8 C2
Carignan F...... 14 A2
Carignano I...... 35 F1
Carling F...... 22 C4
Carmagnola I...... 35 F1
Carmaux F...... 32 B1
Carnac F...... 16 C3
Carpentras F...... 41 D4
Carquefou F...... 17 E2
Carqueiranne F...... 41 F1
Carro F...... 41 D1
Carrouges F...... 10 C1
Carry-le-Rouet F...... 41 D2
Carteret F...... 10 A3
Carvin F...... 13 D4
Casamozza F...... 43 b2
Caselle I...... 35 F2
Cassagnes-Bégonhès F...... 32 B1
Cassel F...... 4 C1
Cassis F...... 41 E2
Casteau B...... 13 E4
Castejón de Sos E...... 37 E1
Casteldelfino I...... 35 E1
Casteljaloux F...... 31 D2
Castellamonte I...... 35 F2
Castellane F...... 42 B3
Castellfollit de la Roca E...... 39 D1
Castelmoron F...... 31 D2
Castelnau-Médoc F...... 30 C4
Castelnau-de-
Montmiral F...... 32 A1
Castelnau-Magnoac F...... 37 F3
Castelnaudary F...... 38 C3
Castelsarrasin F...... 31 E1
Castets F...... 30 A2
Castillon-la-Bataille F...... 31 D3
Castillonnès F...... 31 E3
Castres F...... 39 D3
Castricum NL...... 2 B2
Castries F...... 40 B3
Castrop-Rauxal D...... 7 E2
Catus F...... 31 F2
Caudebec F...... 11 E3
Caudry F...... 13 D3
Caumont F...... 10 B2
Caunes-Minervois F...... 39 D3
Cauro F...... 43 a2
Caussade F...... 31 F1
Cauterets F...... 37 E2
Cauville F...... 11 D3
Cavaillon F...... 41 D3
Cavalaire-sur-Mer F...... 42 A1
Cavalière F...... 42 A1
Cavour F...... 35 F1
Caylus F...... 32 A2

Cazals F...... 31 F3
Cazères F...... 38 B3
Celle Ligure I...... 43 E4
Centuri F...... 43 b3
Cerbère F...... 39 E1
Ceresole Reale I...... 35 F3
Céret F...... 39 D1
Cérilly F...... 26 C3
Cerisiers F...... 20 C3
Cerizay F...... 18 A1
Cernay F...... 23 D1
Cervera del
Rio Alhama E...... 36 A1
Cervione F...... 43 b2
Cesana Torinese I...... 35 E2
Cestona E...... 36 A3
Ceva I...... 43 D4
Ceyzériat F...... 28 A1
Chabanais F...... 25 D2
Chabeuil F...... 34 B2
Chablis F...... 21 D2
Chabreloche F...... 27 D1
Chabris F...... 19 E1
Chagny F...... 27 F3
Chaillé-les-Marais F...... 24 B3
Chalabre F...... 38 C2
Chalais F...... 31 D4
Chalamont F...... 28 A1
Chalampé F...... 23 D1
Challans F...... 17 E1
Challes-les-Eaux F...... 35 D3
Chalon-sur-Saône F...... 28 A3
Chalonnes F...... 18 A2
Châlons-en-
Champagne F...... 21 E4
Châlus F...... 25 E1
Chambéry F...... 34 C3
Chambley-Bussières F...... 22 B4
Chambon-sur-Lac F...... 33 D4
Chambon-sur-Voueize F...... 26 B2
Chambord F...... 19 E2
Chamonix-Mont-Blanc F...... 35 E4
Champagne-Mouton F...... 25 D2
Champagnole F...... 28 C2
Champaubert F...... 21 D4
Champdeniers F...... 24 C3
Champeix F...... 33 D4
Champéry CH...... 29 D1
Champex CH...... 35 F4
Champier F...... 34 B3
Champigné F...... 18 B3
Champillon F...... 13 E1
Champlitte F...... 28 B3
Champlon B...... 14 B3
Champtoceaux F...... 17 F2
Chanas F...... 34 B3
Chantelle F...... 26 C2
Chantemerle F...... 35 D2
Chantilly F...... 12 B2
Chantonnay F...... 24 B4
Chaource F...... 21 D2
Chapelle-Royale F...... 19 E3
Charavines F...... 34 C3
Charenton-du-Cher F...... 26 B3
Charleroi B...... 13 F4
Charleville-Mézières F...... 13 F2
Charlieu F...... 27 E1
Charly F...... 12 C1
Charmes F...... 22 B2
Charny F...... 20 B2
Charolles F...... 27 E1
Chârost F...... 26 B4
Charroux F...... 25 D2
Chartres F...... 19 E4
Chassigny F...... 21 F1
Château d'Oex CH...... 29 E1
Château-Arnoux F...... 41 F4
Château-Chinon F...... 27 E3
Château-du-Loir F...... 18 C3
Château-Gontier F...... 18 B3
Château-la-Vallière F...... 18 C2
Château-Porcien F...... 13 E2
Château-Queyras F...... 35 E1
Château-Renault F...... 19 D2

47

Château-Salins F 22 C3
Château-Thierry F 13 D1
Châteaubourg F 17 F4
Châteaubriant F 17 F3
Châteaudun F 19 E3
Châteaugiron F 17 F4
Châteaulin F 8 B2
Châteaumeillant F 26 B3
Châteauneuf F 24 C1
Châteauneuf-de-
Randon F 33 E2
Châteauneuf-du-Faou F 8 C2
Châteauneuf-du-Pape F 41 D4
Châteauneuf-en-
Thymerais F 19 E4
Chateauneuf-sur-Cher F 26 B3
Châteauneuf-sur-Loire F 20 A2
Châteauneuf-sur-
Sarthe F 18 B3
Châteauponsac F 25 E2
Châteaurenard F 20 B2
Châteauroux F 26 A3
Châteauvillain F 21 E2
Châtel F 29 D1
Châtel-St-Denis CH 29 D2
Châtelaillon-Plage F 24 A3
Châtelet B 13 F4
Châtelguyon F 26 C1
Châtellerault F 25 E4
Châtelus-Malvaleix F 26 A2
Châtenois F 22 B2
Chatham GB 4 A3
Châtillon F 35 F3
Châtillon-Coligny F 20 B2
Châtillon-en-Bazois F 27 D3
Châtillon-en-Diois F 34 B1
Châtillon-sur-
Chalaronne F 27 F1
Châtillon-sur-Indre F 25 F4
Châtillon-sur-Loire F 20 B2
Châtillon-sur-Marne F 13 D1
Châtillon-sur-Seine F 21 E2
Chaudes-Aigues F 33 D2
Chauffailles F 27 E1
Chaufour-lès-
Bonnières F 11 F1
Chaumergy F 28 B3
Chaumont F 19 E2
Chaumont F 21 F2
Chaunay F 25 D3
Chauny F 13 D2
Chaussin F 28 B3
Chauvigny F 25 E3
Chazelles F 34 A4
Chef-Boutonne F 24 C3
Chelmsford GB 4 A4
Chemillé F 18 A2
Chemin F 28 B3
Chénérailles F 26 B2
Chenonceaux F 19 D2
Cherbourg F 10 B4
Chéroy F 20 B3
Chevagnes F 27 D2
Chevanceaux F 24 B1
Chevreuse F 20 A4
Chieri I 35 F2
Chimay B 13 E3
Chinon F 18 C1
Chiusa di Pesio I 43 D4
Cholet F 18 A2
Chorges F 35 D1
Choye F 28 C4
Ciboure F 36 B3
Cierp-Gaud F 37 F2
Ciney B 14 B3
Cintegabelle F 38 C3
Cintruénigo E 36 A1
Cirey F 23 D3
Cirié I 35 F2
Civray F 25 D2
Civrieux-d'Azergues F 34 B4
Clacton-on-Sea GB 4 B4
Clairvaux-les-Lacs F 28 B2
Clamecy F 20 C1

Clavières I 35 E2
Clécy F 10 C2
Clefmont F 22 A2
Clelles F 34 C2
Clères F 11 F3
Clermont F 12 B2
Clermont-en-Argonne F 21 F4
Clermont-Ferrand F 26 C1
Clermont-l'Hérault F 40 A3
Clerval CH 29 D3
Clervaux L 14 C2
Cléry F 19 F2
Cliffe GB 4 A3
Clisson F 17 F2
Cloyes-sur-le-Loir F 19 E3
Cluny F 27 F2
Cluses F 35 E4
Cochem D 15 E2
Coesfeld D 7 E3
Coevorden NL 3 E2
Coggeshall GB 4 A4
Cognac F 24 B2
Cogolin F 42 A2
Colchester GB 4 A4
Coligny F 28 B2
Collinée F 9 E1
Collioure F 39 E1
Colonges F 28 B1
Colmar F 23 D2
Colmars F 42 B4
Cologne F 38 B4
Colombey-les-Belles F 22 B3
Colombey-les-Deux-
Églises F 21 E2
Combeaufontaine F 22 B1
Combourg F 9 F1
Combronde F 26 C1
Commentry F 26 C2
Commercy F 22 B3
Compiègne F 12 C2
Comps-sur-Artuby F 42 B3
Concarneau F 8 B1
Conches F 11 E2
Condat F 32 C3
Condé-en-Brie F 13 D1
Condé-sur-Noireau F 10 C2
Condom F 31 D1
Condrieu F 34 A3
Conflans F 22 B4
Confolens F 25 D2
Conlie F 18 C3
Connerré F 19 D3
Conques F 32 B2
Contay F 12 C3
Contres F 19 E2
Contrexéville F 22 B2
Conty F 12 B3
Coray F 8 B1
Corbeil-Essonnes F 20 B4
Corbie F 12 C3
Corbigny F 27 D4
Corcieux F 22 C2
Cordes F 32 A1
Corella E 36 A1
Corlay F 9 D1
Cormainville F 19 F3
Cormeilles F 11 D2
Cormery F 19 D1
Cornimont F 22 C1
Corps F 34 C2
Corte F 43 b2
Cortemilia I 43 E4
Cosne F 20 B1
Cosne d'Allier F 26 C2
Cossé-le-Vivien F 18 A3
Cossonay CH 29 D2
Cotignac F 41 F2
Couches F 27 F3
Coucy F 13 D2
Couhé F 25 D3
Couilly F 12 C1
Couiza F 39 D2
Coulommiers F 20 C4

Coulon F 24 B3
Coulonges F 24 B3
Couptrain F 10 C1
Cour-Cheverny F 19 E2
Courchevel F 35 E3
Courçon F 24 B3
Courmayeur I 35 E3
Courpière F 33 E4
Courseulles-sur-Mer F 10 C3
Courson-les-Carrières F 20 C1
Courteilles F 11 D2
Courtenay F 20 B2
Courtomer F 11 D1
Courtrai (Kortrijk) B 5 D1
Courville F 19 E4
Coutances F 10 A2
Couterne F 10 C1
Coutevroult F 20 C4
Coutras F 31 D4
Couvet CH 29 D2
Couvin B 13 F3
Cozes F 24 B2
Crans CH 29 E1
Craon F 18 A3
Craponne-sur-Arzon F 33 E3
Crêches-sur-Saône F 27 F1
Crécy F 20 C4
Crécy-en-Ponthieu F 12 B4
Crécy-sur-Serre F 13 D2
Creil F 12 B2
Crémieu F 34 B4
Créon F 30 C3
Crépy-en-Valois F 12 C2
Crespin F 13 E4
Cressensac F 32 A3
Crest F 34 B2
Creutzwald F 22 C4
Crevecoeur F 12 B2
Crissolo I 35 E1
Crocq F 26 B1
Crozon F 8 B2
Cruas F 34 A2
Cruseilles F 35 D4
Cruzy F 39 E3
Cuers F 41 F2
Cuijk NL 6 C3
Cuiseaux F 28 B2
Cuisery F 28 A2
Culan F 26 B3
Culemborg NL 6 C3
Culoz F 34 C4
Cúneo I 43 D4
Cuorgnè I 35 F2
Cusset F 27 D2
Cuvilly F 12 C2

D

Dabo F 23 D3
Dahn D 23 E4
Dammartin-en-Goële F 12 C1
Dampierre F 28 B3
Dampierre-sur-
Boutonne F 24 C3
Dampierre-sur-Salon F 28 C4
Damville F 11 E1
Damvillers F 14 B1
Dangé-St-Romain F 25 E4
Dannemarie F 29 E4
Daoulas F 8 B2
Därligen CH 29 F2
Darney F 22 B2
Dasburg D 14 C2
Datteln D 7 F2
Daun D 15 D3
Dax F 30 A1
De Cocksdorp NL 2 B3
De Haan B 5 D2
De Koog NL 2 B3
De Kooy NL 2 B3

De Panne B 5 D2
Deal GB 4 B3
Deauville F 11 D3
Decazeville F 32 B2
Decize F 27 D3
Dedemsvaart NL 3 E2
Deidesheim D 23 F4
Deinze B 5 E2
Delden NL 7 E4
Delémont CH 29 E3
Delft NL 6 A3
Delfzijl NL 3 E3
Delle F 29 E4
Delme F 22 C3
Den Burg NL 2 B3
Den Haag NL 6 A4
Den Helder NL 2 B3
Den Oever NL 2 C3
Denain F 13 D4
Dendermonde B 5 F2
Denekamp NL 3 E1
Denzlingen D 23 E1
Derval F 17 E3
Descartes F 25 E4
Desvres F 4 B1
Deurne NL 6 C2
Deva E 36 A4
Deventer NL 7 D4
Die F 34 B2
Diekirch L 14 C2
Dieppe F 11 F3
Dierdorf D 15 F3
Dieren NL 7 D3
Diest B 6 B1
Dieulefit F 34 B1
Dieulouard F 22 B3
Dieuze F 22 C3
Diever NL 3 D3
Diez D 15 F3
Differdange L 14 B1
Digne-les-Bains F 42 A3
Digoin F 27 E2
Dijon F 28 A4
Diksmuide B 5 D2
Dillingen D 15 D1
Dinan F 9 E1
Dinant B 14 A3
Dinard F 9 F2
Dinozé F 22 C2
Dinslaken D 7 E2
Dives-sur-Mer F 11 D2
Divonne-les-Bains F 28 C1
Dobel D 23 F3
Doesburg NL 7 D3
Doetinchem NL 7 D3
Dogliani I 43 D4
Dokkum NL 3 D4
Dol-de-Bretagne F 9 F2
Dole F 28 B3
Dombasle F 22 C3
Dombrot-le-Sec F 22 B2
Domburg NL 5 E3
Domèvre-en-Haye F 22 B3
Domfront F 10 B1
Domme F 31 F3
Dompaire F 22 B2
Dompierre F 27 D2
Domrémy-la-Pucelle F 22 B3
Donaueschingen D 23 F1
Donostia/
San Sebastián E 36 B3
Dontilly F 20 C3
Donzenac F 32 A4
Donzère F 34 A1
Donzy F 20 B1
Doorn NL 6 C3
Doornik (Tournai) B 13 D4
Dordives F 20 B3
Dordrecht NL 6 B3
Dormagen D 7 E1
Dormans F 13 D1
Dornes F 27 D3
Dornstetten D 23 F2
Dornum D 3 F4

Dörpen D	3	F3
Dorsten D	7	E2
Dortan F	28	B1
Dortmund D	7	F2
Douai F	13	D4
Douarnenez F	8	B1
Douchy F	20	B2
Doucier F	28	B2
Doudeville F	11	E3
Doué-la-Fontaine F	18	B2
Doulaincourt F	21	F3
Doulevant-le-Château F	21	F3
Doullens F	12	C4
Dourdan F	20	A4
Douvaine F	28	C1
Douzy F	14	A2
Dover GB	4	B2
Dozulé F	11	D2
Drachten NL	3	D3
Draguignan F	42	A2
Drensteinfurt D	7	F2
Dreux F	11	F1
Driebergen NL	6	C3
Dronero I	42	C4
Dronten NL	2	C2
Drusenheim F	23	E3
Druten NL	6	C3
Ducey F	10	A2
Duclair F	11	E3
Dudelange L	14	C1
Düdingen CH	29	E2
Duingt F	35	D4
Duisburg D	7	E2
Dülken D	7	D2
Dülmen D	7	F3
Dun F	14	A1
Dun-le-Palestel F	25	F2
Dun-sur-Auron F	26	C3
Dunkerque F	4	C2
Dunkerque Ouest F	4	C2
Duras F	31	D3
Durban-Corbières F	39	E2
Durbuy B	14	B3
Düren D	15	D4
Durtal F	18	B3
Düsseldorf D	7	E1
Dwingeloo NL	3	E3
Dymchurch GB	4	A2

E

Earl's Colne GB	4	A4
Eaux-Bonnes F	37	D2
Eaux-Chaudes F	37	D2
Eauze F	30	C1
Ebreuil F	26	C2
Echallens CH	29	D2
Echallon F	28	B1
Echarri/Aranaz E	36	A3
Echternach L	14	C2
Ecommoy F	18	C3
Ecouis F	11	F2
Ecueillé F	25	F4
Ecury F	21	E4
Edam NL	2	C2
Ede NL	6	C3
Edenkoben D	23	F4
Eeklo B	5	E2
Eghezée B	14	A4
Egletons F	32	B4
Egmond aan Zee NL	2	B2
Eguzon F	25	F3
Ehnen L	14	C2
Eibar E	36	A3
Eibergen NL	7	E3
Eich D	15	F1
Eindhoven NL	6	C2
Eitorf D	15	E4
Ejea de los Caballeros E	36	B1
El Pont de Suert E	37	F1

El Port de la Selva E	39	E1
El Serrat AND	38	B2
El Villar de Arnedo E	36	A2
Elantxobe E	36	A4
Elbeuf F	11	E2
Elburg NL	3	D2
Elgoibar E	36	A3
Elizondo E	36	B3
Elmpt D	7	D1
Elne F	39	E1
Elsdorf D	7	D1
Elst NL	6	C3
Elten D	7	D3
Eltville D	15	F2
Elzach D	23	E2
Embrun F	35	D1
Emden D	3	F3
Emlichheim D	3	E2
Emmeloord NL	3	D2
Emmen D	3	E2
Emmendingen D	23	E2
Emmerich D	7	D3
Emsdetten D	7	F3
Encamp AND	38	B1
Engelskirchen D	15	E4
Engen D	23	F1
Enghien B	5	F1
Englefontaine F	13	E3
Enkhuizen NL	2	C2
Enschede NL	7	E3
Ensisheim F	23	D1
Entlebuch CH	29	F2
Entraygues-sur-Truyère F	32	C2
Entrevaux F	42	B3
Entrèves I	35	E4
Epannes F	24	B3
Epe D	7	E3
Epe NL	3	D2
Épernay F	13	E1
Epernon F	19	F4
Épinal F	22	C2
Epône F	12	A1
Erbalunga F	43	b3
Erftstadt D	15	D4
Erkelenz D	7	D1
Ermelo NL	2	C2
Ermenonville F	12	C1
Ernée F	18	B4
Erquy F	9	E2
Errazu E	36	B3
Erro E	36	B3
Erstein F	23	E2
Ervy-le-Châtel F	21	D2
Escároz E	36	C2
Esch-sur-Alzette L	14	C1
Esch-sur-Sûre L	14	C2
Eschweiler D	15	D4
Espalion F	32	C2
Espelette F	36	C3
Espot E	38	B2
Essen D	7	E2
Estagel F	39	D2
Estaires F	5	D1
Estavayer-le-Lac CH	29	D2
Estella E	36	A2
Esternay F	21	D4
Esterri de Aneu E	38	B2
Esterwegen D	3	F3
Estissac F	21	D3
Estrées-St-Denis F	12	C1
Étables-sur-Mer F	9	D2
Etain F	14	B1
Etalle B	14	B2
Étampes F	20	A4
Étaples F	4	B1
Etretat F	11	D3
Ettelbruck L	14	C2
Ettenheim D	23	E2
Ettlingen D	23	F3
Eu F	12	A4
Eupen B	14	C4
Europoort NL	6	A3
Euskirchen D	15	D4
Evaux-les-Bains F	26	B2

Evian-les-Bains F	29	D1
Evisa F	43	a2
Evolène CH	35	F4
Evran F	9	E1
Evreux F	11	E2
Evron F	18	B4
Evry F	20	B4
Excideuil F	31	F4
Exmes F	11	D1
Eyguières F	41	D3
Eygurande F	26	B1
Eymet F	31	D3
Eymoutiers F	25	F1

F

Falaise F	10	C2
Fanjeaux F	39	D3
Farébersviller F	23	D4
Faucogney-et-la-Mer F	22	C1
Faulensee CH	29	F2
Faulquemont F	22	C4
Fauville F	11	E3
Faverges F	35	D3
Faverney F	22	B1
Faversham GB	4	A3
Fayence F	42	B2
Fayl-Billot F	22	A1
Fécamp F	11	E3
Feldberg D	23	E1
Felixstowe GB	4	B4
Felletin F	26	A1
Fenestrelle I	35	E2
Fénétrange F	23	D3
Fère-Champenoise F	21	D4
Fère-en-Tardenois F	13	D1
Ferrette F	29	E3
Ferrières F	20	B3
Feurs F	33	F4
Fiesch CH	29	F1
Figari F	43	a1
Figeac F	32	B2
Finnentrop D	7	F1
Firminy F	33	F3
Fischbach D	23	E4
Fismes F	13	D1
Fitero E	36	A1
Flaine F	35	E4
Flavigny-sur-Moselle F	22	B3
Flers F	10	C2
Fleurance F	31	D1
Fleuré F	25	D3
Fleurier CH	29	D2
Fleurus B	13	F4
Fleury F	11	F2
Flins F	12	A1
Flize F	13	F2
Flogny-la-Chapelle F	21	D2
Florac F	33	D1
Florennes B	13	F3
Florenville B	14	B2
Flumet F	35	E4
Foix F	38	C2
Folkestone GB	4	A2
Font-Romeu F	38	C1
Fontaine-Française F	28	B4
Fontaine-le-Dun F	11	E3
Fontainebleau F	20	B3
Fontenay-le-Comte F	24	B3
Fontenay-Trésigny F	20	C4
Forbach F	23	D4
Forbach D	23	F3
Forcalquier F	41	E3
Forges-les-Eaux F	12	A3
Formerie F	12	A3
Fornovo F	5	F4
Fos F	38	A2
Fos-sur-Mer F	41	D2
Fossano I	43	D4
Fosses B	14	A3
Foucarmont F	12	A3

Fouesnant F	8	B1
Fougères F	10	A1
Fougerolles F	22	B1
Foulain F	21	F2
Fouras F	24	A3
Fourcès F	31	D1
Fourmies F	13	E3
Fournels F	33	D2
Fours F	27	D3
Frabosa Soprana I	43	D4
Fraize F	23	D2
Francardo F	43	b2
Franeker NL	2	C3
Frangy F	35	D4
Frankenthal D	15	F1
Frayssinet F	32	A2
Frechen D	15	D4
Freiburg im Breisgau D	23	E1
Fréjus F	42	B2
Fresnay-sur-Sarthe F	18	C4
Fresnes F	13	D4
Fresnes F	22	B2
Fresnes-en-Woëvre F	22	B4
Fréteval F	19	E3
Fretigny-et-Velloreille F	28	C4
Freudenberg D	15	E4
Freudenstadt D	23	F2
Frévent F	12	C4
Freyming Merlebach F	23	D4
Fribourg CH	29	E2
Frick D	29	F3
Froissy F	12	B2
Fromental F	10	C1
Frontignan F	40	B3
Frutigen CH	4	C1
Frutigen CH	29	E2
Fuenterrabia/Hondarribia E	36	B4
Fumay F	13	F3
Fumel F	31	E2
Furnes (Veurne) B	5	D2
Fürstenau D	3	F2
Furtwangen D	23	E1

G

Gabarret F	30	C2
Gacé F	11	D1
Gaël F	9	E1
Gaggenau D	23	F3
Gaillac F	39	D4
Gaillon F	11	F2
Gallargues F	40	B3
Gamaches-en-Vexin F	12	A3
Gan F	37	D3
Gand (Gent) B	5	E2
Ganges F	40	B4
Gannat F	26	C2
Gap F	34	C1
Gardanne F	41	E2
Garéssio I	43	D3
Gavarnie F	37	E2
Gavi F	43	F4
Gavray F	10	B2
Gedinne B	14	A3
Geel B	6	B2
Geertruidenberg NL	6	B3
Geilenkirchen D	6	C1
Geisingen D	23	F1
Geldern D	7	D2
Geldrop NL	6	C2
Geleen NL	6	C1
Gelsenkirchen D	7	E2
Gembloux B	14	A4
Gémenos F	41	E2
Gemert NL	6	C2
Gémozac F	24	B2
Gemünd D	15	D3
Gemünden D	15	E2

Genappe B............... 13 F4
Gençay F................... 25 D3
Génelard F................ 27 E2
Genève CH.............. 28 C1
Genk B...................... 6 C1
Genlis F.................... 28 B3
Gennep NL................ 7 D2
Gennes F................... 18 B2
Génolhac F............... 33 E1
Génova I................... 43 F4
Gent (Gand) B......... 5 E2
Gentioux F............... 26 A1
Georgsheil D............ 3 F4
Geraardsbergen B..... 5 E1
Gérardmer F............. 22 C2
Gerbéviller F............ 22 C3
Germay F.................. 22 A3
Germersheim D......... 23 F4
Gernsbach D............. 23 F3
Gerolstein D............. 15 D3
Gescher D................ 7 E3
Gevrey-Chambertin F... 28 A3
Gex F....................... 28 C1
Ghisonaccia F........... 43 b2
Ghisoni F.................. 43 b2
Gien F...................... 20 B2
Giens F..................... 41 F1
Gieten NL................. 3 E3
Giethoorn NL............ 3 D2
Gignac F................... 40 A3
Gillingham GB........... 4 A3
Gimont F.................. 38 B4
Giromagny F............. 22 C1
Gisors F.................... 12 A2
Gistel B.................... 5 D2
Givet F..................... 14 A3
Givors F.................... 34 B3
Givry B..................... 13 E4
Givry F..................... 27 F3
Givry-en-Argonne F... 21 F4
Gizeux F................... 18 C2
Gladbeck D.............. 7 E2
Glénic F.................... 26 A2
Goch D..................... 7 D2
Goderville F............. 11 E3
Goes NL................... 5 F3
Goirle NL.................. 6 B2
Golfe-Juan F............. 42 C2
Golfo di Sogno F....... 43 b1
Goncelin F................ 34 C3
Gondrecourt F.......... 22 A3
Gondrin F................. 31 D1
Goor NL.................... 7 E4
Goppenstein CH....... 29 F1
Gordes F................... 41 D3
Gorinchem NL........... 6 B3
Gorredijk NL............. 3 D3
Gorron F................... 10 B1
Gosselies B.............. 13 F4
Gouarec F................. 9 D1
Gouda NL................. 6 B3
Goumois CH............. 29 E3
Gourdon F................ 31 F3
Gourin F................... 8 C1
Gournay-en-Bray F... 12 A2
Gouzon F.................. 26 B2
Graçay F................... 26 A4
Grächen CH.............. 29 F1
Gramat F.................. 32 A3
Grancey F................. 21 E1
Grand-Champ F........ 17 D4
Grandcamp-Maisy F... 10 B3
Grande-Fougeray F... 17 E3
Grandpré F............... 13 F1
Grandrieu F.............. 33 E2
Grandvilliers F.......... 12 B3
Granges-sur-Vologne F... 22 C2
Granville F................ 10 A2
Grasse F................... 42 B2
Graulhet F................ 39 D4
Grave NL.................. 6 C3
Gravelines F............. 4 C2
Gray F...................... 28 B4
Great Dunmow GB..... 4 A4

Great Yeldham GB...... 4 A4
Greetsiel D............... 3 F4
Grenade F................. 30 B1
Grenade F................. 38 C4
Grenchen CH............ 29 E3
Grenoble F............... 34 C2
Gréoux-les-Bains F... 41 E3
Greven D.................. 7 F3
Grevenbroich D......... 7 D1
Grevenbrück D.......... 7 F1
Grevenmacher L....... 14 C2
Grez-en-Bouère F..... 18 B3
Grignan F.................. 34 A1
Grignols F................. 30 C2
Grimaud F................. 42 A2
Grindelwald CH........ 29 F2
Grisolles F................ 31 E1
Groenlo NL............... 7 E3
Gronau D.................. 7 E3
Groningen NL............ 3 E3
Grosshöchstetten CH... 29 F2
Grostenquin F........... 22 C4
Grouw NL................. 3 D3
Gruissan F................ 39 E2
Grünstadt D.............. 15 F1
Gruyères CH............. 29 E2
Gstaad CH................ 29 E1
Gsteig CH................. 29 E1
Guebwiller F............. 23 D1
Guémené-Penfao F... 17 E3
Guémené-sur-Scorff F... 8 C1
Guer F...................... 17 E4
Guérande F............... 17 D3
Guéret F................... 26 A2
Guérigny F................ 27 D4
Guetaria E................ 36 A4
Guéthary F............... 36 B4
Gueugnon F.............. 27 E2
Guichen F................. 17 E4
Guignes F................. 20 B4
Guillaumes F............ 42 B3
Guillestre F............... 35 D1
Guilvinec F............... 8 B1
Guînes F................... 4 B2
Guingamp F.............. 9 D2
Guipry F................... 17 E3
Guîtres F.................. 13 D3
Guitres F.................. 31 D4
Gujan-Mestras F....... 30 B3
Gummersbach D........ 7 F1
Gunten CH............... 29 F2
Guntersblum D......... 15 F2
Gwatt CH................. 29 E2
Gy F......................... 28 C4

Hardenberg NL.......... 3 E2
Harderwijk NL........... 2 C2
Haren NL.................. 3 E3
Haren D.................... 3 F2
Haren NL.................. 3 E3
Harfleur F................. 11 D3
Harlingen NL............. 2 C3
Haroué F.................. 22 B3
Harwich GB.............. 4 B4
Haselünne D............. 3 F2
Haslach D................. 23 E2
Hasparren F............. 36 C3
Hasselt B.................. 6 B1
Hasselt NL................ 3 D2
Hattem NL................ 3 D2
Hattingen D.............. 7 E2
Hausach D................ 23 E2
Häusern D................ 23 E1
Haut-Asco F............. 43 a2
Haute-Nendaz CH..... 35 F4
Hauteville Plage F..... 10 A2
Havelange B............. 14 B3
Hawkinge GB............ 4 A2
Hayange F................ 14 C1
Hazebrouck F........... 4 C1
Headcorn GB............ 4 A3
Hechtel B.................. 6 B1
Hédé F..................... 9 F1
Heek D..................... 7 E3
Heemstede NL.......... 2 B2
Heerde NL................ 3 D2
Heerenveen NL......... 3 D3
Heerlen NL............... 6 C1
Heeze NL.................. 6 C2
Heiden D.................. 7 E3
Heino NL.................. 3 D2
Heinsberg D............. 7 D1
Hellendoorn NL......... 3 D2
Hellevoetsluis NL...... 6 A3
Helmond NL............. 6 C2
Hemer D................... 7 F2
Hèming F.................. 23 D3
Hendaye F................ 36 B3
Hengelo NL............... 7 E4
Hénin Beaumont F.... 13 D4
Hennebont F............. 16 C4
Henrichemont F........ 20 A1
Herbault F................ 19 E2
Herbesthal B............ 14 C4
Herbeumont B.......... 14 B2
Herentals B.............. 6 B2
Héricourt F............... 29 D4
Hérisson F................ 26 C3
Herment F................ 26 B1
Hermeskeil D........... 15 D1
Herne D.................... 7 E2
Herne Bay GB........... 4 B3
Herselt B.................. 6 B1
Herzlake D............... 3 F2
Hesdin F................... 12 B4
Hesel D.................... 3 F3
Hettange-Grande F... 14 C1
Heyrieux F............... 34 B3
Hiersac F.................. 24 C2
Hilchenbach D.......... 15 F4
Hilden D................... 7 E1
Hillegom NL.............. 2 B2
Hilterfingen CH........ 29 E2
Hilvarenbeek NL....... 6 B2
Hilversum NL............ 2 C1
Hinterweidenthal D... 23 E4
Hinterzarten D......... 23 E1
Hirsingue F.............. 29 E4
Hirson F................... 13 E3
Höchenschwand D... 23 E1
Hochfelden F............ 23 E3
Hochspeyer D.......... 15 F1
Hockenheim D.......... 23 F4
Hoedekenskerke NL... 5 F2
Hoek van Holland NL... 6 A3
Hohenlimburg D....... 7 F2
Hollum NL................ 3 D4
Holten NL................. 7 D4

Holwerd NL.............. 3 D4
Homburg D............... 23 D4
Homps F................... 39 E3
Hondarriba/
  Fuenterrabia E...... 36 B4
Honfleur F................ 11 D3
Hoogerheide NL....... 6 A2
Hoogeveen NL.......... 3 E2
Hoogezand NL.......... 3 E3
Hoogkarspel NL........ 2 C2
Hoogstraten B.......... 6 B2
Hoorn NL.................. 2 C2
Hopsten D................ 7 F4
Horb D..................... 23 F2
Hordain F................. 13 D4
Hornberg D.............. 23 F2
Hornoy F.................. 12 B3
Horst NL.................. 7 D2
Hörstel D.................. 7 F3
Horstmar D.............. 7 F3
Hossegor F............... 30 A1
Hostens F................. 30 C3
Hotton B.................. 14 B3
Houdain F................ 12 C4
Houdan F................. 11 F1
Houdelaincourt F...... 22 A3
Houeillès F............... 30 C2
Houffalize B............. 14 B3
Houlgate F............... 11 D3
Hourtin F................. 24 A1
Hourtin-Plage F........ 24 A1
Hucqueliers F........... 4 B1
Huelgoat F............... 8 C2
Hüfingen D............... 23 F1
Huizen NL................ 2 B2
Huizen NL................ 2 C2
Hulst NL.................. 5 F2
Huriel F.................... 26 B2
Huttwil CH............... 29 F3
Huy B....................... 14 B4
Hyères F................... 41 F1
Hythe GB................. 4 A2

I

Ibbenbüren D........... 7 F3
Iciar E...................... 36 A3
Idar-Oberstein D...... 15 E2
Idstein D.................. 15 F2
Ieper (Ypres) B........ 5 D1
IJmuiden NL............. 2 B2
Illiers F.................... 19 E3
Imphy F.................... 27 D3
Ingelheim D.............. 15 F2
Ingelmunster B......... 5 D1
Ingwiller F................ 23 D3
Innertkirchen CH...... 29 F2
Ins CH..................... 29 E3
Interlaken CH........... 29 F2
Ipswich GB............... 4 B4
Irun E...................... 36 B3
Iruña/Pamplona E... 36 B2
Irurita E................... 36 B3
Irurzun E.................. 36 B3
Is-sur-Tille F............ 28 B4
Isaba E.................... 36 C2
Isdes F..................... 20 A2
Iselle I..................... 29 F1
Iserlohn D................ 7 F2
Isigny F.................... 10 B3
Isola F..................... 42 C4
Isola 2000 F............. 42 C3
Isona E.................... 38 A1
Isselburg D.............. 7 D3
Issoire F.................. 33 D4
Issoudun F............... 26 B4
Istres F.................... 41 D3
Itxassou F................ 36 C3
Ivry-la-Bataille F...... 11 F1
Izegem B.................. 5 D1

50

Izernore F....... 28 B1

J

Jaca E....... 37 D1
Jaligny-sur-Besbre F....... 27 D2
Janville F....... 19 F3
Janzé F....... 17 F4
Jard-sur-Mer F....... 24 A4
Jargeau F....... 20 A2
Jarnac F....... 24 C2
Jarnages F....... 26 A2
Jarny F....... 22 B4
Jaun CH....... 29 E2
Jausiers F....... 42 B4
Javron F....... 18 C4
Jeumont F....... 13 E3
Jodoigne B....... 14 A4
Joigny F....... 20 C2
Joinville F....... 21 F3
Jonzac F....... 24 B1
Josselin F....... 17 D4
Jougne F....... 28 C2
Joure NL....... 3 D3
Joyeuse F....... 33 E1
Juan-les-Pins F....... 42 C2
Jugon-les-Lacs F....... 9 E1
Juillac F....... 32 A4
Juist D....... 3 F4
Jülich D....... 7 D1
Jullouville F....... 10 A2
Jumeaux F....... 33 D4
Jumièges F....... 11 E2
Juniville F....... 13 E1
Jussey F....... 22 B1
Juvigny-le-Tertre F....... 10 B2
Juzennecourt F....... 21 F2

K

Kaatsheuvel NL....... 6 B3
Kaisersesch D....... 15 E3
Kaiserslautern D....... 15 E1
Kalkar D....... 7 D3
Kamen D....... 7 F2
Kamp Lintfort D....... 7 D2
Kampen NL....... 3 D2
Kandel D....... 23 F4
Kandern D....... 29 F4
Kandersteg CH....... 29 E1
Karlsruhe D....... 23 F3
Kastellaun D....... 15 E2
Kasterlee B....... 6 B2
Katwijk aan Zee NL....... 2 A2
Kaub D....... 15 F2
Kaysersberg F....... 23 D2
Kehl D....... 23 E3
Kelberg D....... 15 D3
Kempen D....... 7 D2
Kenzingen D....... 23 E2
Kerken D....... 7 D2
Kerkrade NL....... 14 C4
Kerpen D....... 15 D4
Kerzers CH....... 29 E2
Kettwig D....... 7 E2
Kevelaer D....... 7 D2
Kiental CH....... 29 F2
Kingsdown GB....... 4 B2
Kirchberg D....... 15 E2
Kirchheimbolanden D....... 15 F1
Kirchundem D....... 15 F4
Kirn D....... 15 E2
Klazienaveen NL....... 3 E2
Kleve D....... 7 D3
Kniebis D....... 23 F2
Knokke-Heist B....... 5 E2

Koblenz D....... 15 E3
Koksijde-Bad B....... 5 D2
Köln D....... 15 E4
Königsfeld D....... 23 F2
Königswinter D....... 15 E4
Köniz CH....... 29 E2
Konz D....... 15 D2
Kortrijk (Courtrai) B....... 5 D1
Kotten NL....... 7 E3
Kranenburg D....... 7 D3
Krefeld D....... 7 D2
Kreuztal D....... 15 F4
Krimpen aan den
IJssel NL....... 6 B3
Kruiningen NL....... 5 F2
Kusel D....... 15 E1
Kyllburg D....... 15 D2

L

L'Aber-Wrac'h F....... 8 B3
L'Aigle F....... 11 E1
L'Aiguillon F....... 24 A3
L'Alpe-d'Huez F....... 35 D2
L'Arbresle F....... 34 A4
L'Argentière-la-Bessée F....... 35 D1
L'Echalp F....... 35 E1
L'Escarène F....... 42 C3
L'Isle-Adam F....... 12 B1
L'Isle-de-Noé F....... 37 F3
L'Isle-en-Dodon F....... 38 B3
L'Isle-Jourdain F....... 38 B4
L'Isle-Jourdain F....... 25 D3
L'Isle-sur-la-Sorgue F....... 41 D3
L'Isle-sur-le-Doubs F....... 29 D4
L'Ile-Bouchard F....... 18 C1
L'Ile-Rousse F....... 43 a3
La Bassée F....... 12 C4
La Bastide de-Sérou F....... 38 B3
La Bastide-Puylaurent F....... 33 E2
La Bâtie-Neuve F....... 35 D1
La Baule F....... 17 D3
La Bazoche-Gouet F....... 19 E3
La Belle Etoile F....... 21 D3
La Bérarde F....... 35 D2
La Bourboule F....... 32 C4
La Bresse F....... 22 C1
La Brillanne F....... 41 F3
La Canourgue F....... 33 D2
La Capelle F....... 13 E3
La Capte F....... 41 F1
La Cavalerie F....... 39 F4
La Celle-Dunoise F....... 26 A2
La Chaise-Dieu F....... 33 E3
La Chambre F....... 35 D3
La Chapelle F....... 27 F1
La Chapelle-d'Angillon F....... 20 A1
La Chapelle-en-
Vercors F....... 34 B2
La Chapelle-Glain F....... 17 F3
La Charité-sur-Loire F....... 26 C4
La Chartre F....... 19 D2
La Châtaigneraie F....... 24 B4
La Châtre F....... 26 A3
La Chaux-de-Fonds CH....... 29 D3
La Ciotat F....... 41 E2
La Clayette F....... 27 E2
La Clusaz F....... 35 D4
La Cluse F....... 28 B1
La Cluse-et-Mijoux F....... 28 C2
La Coquille F....... 25 E1
La Côte-St-André F....... 34 B3
La Courtine F....... 26 B1
La Croisière F....... 25 F2
La Croix-Valmer F....... 42 B2
La Croixille F....... 18 A4
La Cure F....... 28 C2
La Fère F....... 13 D2
La Ferté-Bernard F....... 19 D3
La Ferté-Gaucher F....... 20 C4

La Ferté-Macé F....... 10 C1
La Ferté-Milon F....... 12 C1
La Ferté-St-Aubin F....... 19 F2
La Ferté-sous-Jouarre F....... 12 C1
La Ferté-Vidame F....... 11 E1
La Flèche F....... 18 C3
La Flotte F....... 24 A3
La Gacilly F....... 17 E3
La Garde-Freinet F....... 42 A2
La Grand-Combe F....... 33 E1
La Grande-Motte F....... 40 B3
La Grave F....... 35 D2
La Guerche F....... 26 C3
La Guerche-de-
Bretagne F....... 18 A3
La Haye-du-Puits F....... 10 A3
La Hutte F....... 18 C4
La Javie F....... 42 A4
La Jonquera E....... 39 E1
La Loupe F....... 19 E4
La Louvière B....... 13 E4
La Machine F....... 27 D3
La Malène F....... 33 D1
La Maucarrière F....... 24 C4
La Molina E....... 38 C1
La Mongie F....... 37 E2
La Mothe-Achard F....... 17 E1
La Motte-Chalancon F....... 34 B1
La Mure F....... 34 C2
La Napoule-Plage F....... 42 B2
La Neuve-Lyre F....... 11 E1
La Neuveville CH....... 29 E3
La Pacaudière F....... 27 D1
La Pallice F....... 24 A3
La Palmyre F....... 24 A2
La Palud-sur-Verdon F....... 42 A3
La Petite-Pierre F....... 23 D3
La Plagne F....... 35 E3
La Pobla de Segur E....... 38 A1
La Réole F....... 31 D3
La Roche-Bernard F....... 17 D3
La Roche-Chalais F....... 31 D4
La Roche-en-Ardenne B....... 14 B3
La Roche-Posay F....... 25 E4
La Roche-sur-Foron F....... 35 D4
La Roche-sur-Yon F....... 17 E1
La Rochefoucauld F....... 25 D2
La Rochelle F....... 24 A3
La Rochette F....... 35 D3
La Roque-Gageac F....... 31 F3
La Roquebrussanne F....... 41 F2
La Salvetat F....... 32 B1
La Salvetat-sur-Agout F....... 39 E3
La Seu d'Urgell E....... 38 B1
La Seyne F....... 41 E2
La Souterraine F....... 25 F2
La Suze-sur-Sarthe F....... 18 C3
La Thuile I....... 35 E3
La Tour-du-Pin F....... 34 C3
La Tranche-sur-Mer F....... 24 A3
La Tremblade F....... 24 A2
La Trimouille F....... 25 E3
La Trinité F....... 16 C3
La Trinité-Porhoët F....... 9 D1
La Turbie F....... 42 C3
La Voulte-sur-Rhône F....... 34 A2
La Wantzenau F....... 23 E3
Laarbruch D....... 7 D2
Labastide-d'Armagnac F....... 30 C2
Labastide-Murat F....... 32 A2
Labenne F....... 30 A1
Labouheyre F....... 30 B2
Labrède F....... 30 C3
Labrit F....... 30 B2
Lacanau F....... 30 B4
Lacanau-Océan F....... 30 B4
Lacapelle-Marival F....... 32 B2
Lacaune F....... 39 E4
Lacq F....... 37 D3
Ladbergen D....... 7 F3
Ladon F....... 20 B2
Laferté F....... 22 A1
Laffrey F....... 34 C2
Lafrançaise F....... 31 E1

Lagnieu F....... 34 C4
Lagny F....... 12 C1
Lagrasse F....... 39 E2
Laguépie F....... 32 A1
Laguiole F....... 32 C2
Lahnstein D....... 15 E3
Lahr D....... 23 E2
Laignes F....... 21 D2
Laissac F....... 32 C2
Lalinde F....... 31 E3
Lalouvesc F....... 34 A3
Lamalou-les-Bains F....... 39 E3
Lamarche F....... 22 B2
Lambrecht D....... 23 F4
Lamarque F....... 30 C4
Lamastre F....... 34 A2
Lamballe F....... 9 E2
Lambesc F....... 41 D3
Lamotte-Beuvron F....... 19 F2
Lampaul-Plouarzel F....... 8 A2
Lamure-sur-Azergues F....... 27 E1
Landau D....... 23 F4
Landerneau F....... 8 B2
Landévennec F....... 8 B2
Landivisiau F....... 8 B2
Landivy F....... 10 B1
Landrecies F....... 13 E3
Landstuhl D....... 15 E1
Langeac F....... 33 D3
Langeais F....... 18 C2
Langenfeld D....... 7 E1
Langenhahn D....... 15 F3
Langenthal CH....... 29 F3
Langeoog D....... 3 F4
Langnau im
Emmental CH....... 29 F2
Langogne F....... 33 E2
Langoiran F....... 30 C3
Langon F....... 30 C3
Langres F....... 21 F2
Lanmeur F....... 8 C2
Lannemezan F....... 37 F2
Lannilis F....... 8 B3
Lannoy F....... 8 C2
Lanouaille F....... 31 F4
Lanslebourg-
Mont-Cenis F....... 35 E2
Lantosque F....... 42 C3
Lanvollon F....... 9 D2
Lanzo Torinese I....... 35 F2
Laon F....... 13 D2
Lapalisse F....... 27 D2
Laplume F....... 31 D2
Lapoutroie F....... 23 D2
Laqueuille F....... 32 C4
Laragne-Montéglin F....... 41 F4
Larche F....... 32 A3
Larche F....... 42 B4
Largentière F....... 33 F1
Lari F....... 41 b3
Larmor F....... 16 C4
Larochette L....... 14 C2
Laroque-des-Arcs F....... 31 F2
Laroquebrou F....... 32 B3
Larrau F....... 36 C2
Laruns F....... 37 D2
Las Campanas E....... 36 B2
Lassay F....... 10 C1
Lassigny F....... 12 C2
Lathen D....... 3 F2
Laubrières F....... 18 A3
Laufen CH....... 29 E3
Laufenburg D....... 29 F4
Laufenburg CH....... 29 F3
Laugnac F....... 29 F2
Laurière F....... 25 F2
Lausanne CH....... 29 D2
Lauterbourg F....... 23 F3
Lauterbrunnen CH....... 29 F1
Lauterecken D....... 15 E1
Lautrec F....... 39 D4
Lauwersoog NL....... 3 D4
Lauzerte F....... 31 E2
Lauzun F....... 31 D3

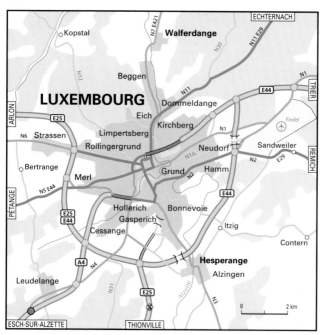

Map labels: ECHTERNACH, Kopstal, Walferdange, N7 E421, N11 E29, N30, N1, Beggen, N11, TRIER, E44, LUXEMBOURG, Dommeldange, ARLON, E25, Eich, Kirchberg, Findel, N6, Strassen, Limpertsberg, N1, N12, Rollingergrund, Neudorf, Sandweiler, REMICH, N1A, N2, E29, Bertrange, Merl, Grund, Hamm, N2, PÉTANGE, N5 E44, E44, Hollerich, Bonnevoie, E25, E44, Gasperich, Itzig, Cessange, Contern, A4, N4, Hesperange, Leudelange, Alzingen, N31, E25, N3, Alzette, 0 2 km, ESCH-SUR-ALZETTE, THIONVILLE

Laval F	18	B4	Le Luc F	42	A2	Roussillon F	34	A3
Lavardac F	31	D2	Le Ludd F	18	C2	Lebach D	15	D1
Lavaur F	38	C4	Le Mans F	18	C3	Lectoure F	31	D1
Lavelanet F	38	C2	Le Markstein F	23	D1	Lédignan F	40	B4
Lavoûte-Chilhac F	33	D3	Le Mas-d'Azil F	38	B3	Leek NL	3	E3
Lavoûte-sur-Loire F	33	E3	Le Mayet F	27	D1	Leer D	3	F3
Le Bar F	42	B3	Le Merlerault F	11	D1	Leerdam NL	6	B3
Le Barp F	30	B3	Le Monastier F	33	E2	Leeuwarden NL	3	D3
Le Beausset F	41	E2	Le Monêtier-les-Bains F	35	D2	Legden D	7	E3
Le Blanc F	25	E3	Le Mont-Dore F	33	D4	Legé F	17	E2
Le Boulou F	39	E1	Le Mont-St-Michel F	10	A2	Léguevin F	38	B4
Le Bourg d'Oisans F	34	C2	Le Montet F	26	C2	Leiden NL	2	B1
Le Bourget F	34	C3	Le Muret F	30	B3	Leissigen CH	29	F2
Le Bugue F	31	E3	Le Muy F	42	B2	Lekeitio E	36	A4
Le Cap-d'Agde F	40	A2	Le Neubourg F	11	E2	Lekunberri E	36	B3
Le Cateau-Cambrésis F	13	D3	Le Nouvion-en-			Lelystad NL	2	C2
Le Catelet F	13	D3	Thiérache F	13	E3	Lembach F	23	E3
Le Caylar F	40	A4	Le Palais F	16	C3	Lembeye F	37	E3
Le Chateau-d'Oléron F	24	A2	Le Perthus F	39	E1	Lemmer NL	3	D3
Le Châtelard F	35	D3	Le Pin-au-Haras F	11	D1	Lempdes F	33	D3
Le Châtelet F	26	B3	Le Poiré-sur-Vie F	17	E1	Lempdes F	26	C1
Le Chesne F	13	F2	Le Pont-de-Beauvoisin F	34	C3	Lencloître F	25	D4
Le Cheylard F	33	F2	Le Pont-de-Claix F	34	C2	Lenk CH	29	E1
Le Conquet F	8	A2	Le Pontet F	24	B1	Lens F	12	C4
Le Creusot F	27	E3	Le Portel F	4	B1	Lenzkirch D	23	E1
Le Croisic F	17	D3	Le Pouldu F	16	B4	Léon F	30	A2
Le Crotoy F	12	A4	Le Pouzin F	34	A2	Leopoldsburg B	6	B1
Le Donjon F	27	D2	Le Puy F	33	E3	Lés E	37	F1
Le Dorat F	25	E2	Le Quesnoy F	13	E3	Les Abrets F	34	C3
Le Faou F	8	B2	Le Rabot F	19	F2	Les Adrets F	42	B2
Le Faouët F	8	C1	Le Rozier F	33	D1	Les Aix-d'Angillon F	26	C4
Le Fossat F	38	B3	Le Russey F	29	D3	Les Andelys F	11	F2
Le Grand-Bourg F	25	F2	Le Teil F	34	A1	Les Arcs F	35	E3
Le Grand-Lucé F	19	D3	Le Teilleul F	10	B1	Les Arcs F	42	A2
Le Grand-Pressigny F	25	E4	Le Thillot F	22	C1	Les Baux-de-Provence F	41	D3
Le Grau-du-Roi F	40	B3	Le Touquet-Paris-Plage F	4	B1	Les Cabannes F	38	C2
Le Havre F	11	D3	Le Touvet F	34	C3	Les Contamines-		
Le Hohwald F	23	D2	Le Trayas F	42	B2	Montjoie F	35	E4
Le Lauzet-Ubaye F	42	B4	Le Tréport F	12	A4	Les Deux-Alpes F	35	D2
Le Lavandou F	42	A1	Le Val-André F	9	E2	Les Diablerets CH	29	E1
Le Lion-d'Angers F	18	B3	Le Vaudreuil F	11	F2	Les Echarmeaux F	27	E1
Le Locle CH	29	D3	Le Verdon F	24	A2	Les Echelles F	34	C3
Le Logis-du-Pin F	42	B3	Le Vernet F	42	B4	Les Epesses F	18	A1
Le Loroux-Bottereau F	17	F2	Le Vigan F	40	B4	Les Escaldes AND	38	B1
Le Louroux F	18	A3	Le-Péage-de-			Les Essarts F	17	F1

Les Eyzies-de-Tayac F	31	F3
Les Gets F	29	D1
Les Halles F	34	A4
Les Haudères CH	35	F4
Les Hayons F	11	F3
Les Herbiers F	17	F1
Les Houches F	35	E4
Les Issambres F	42	B2
Les Laumes F	21	E1
Les Lecques F	41	E2
Les Menuires F	35	D3
Les Pieux F	10	A4
Les Planches-en-		
Montagne F	28	C2
Les Ponts-de-Cé F	18	B2
Les Riceys F	21	D2
Les Rosiers F	18	B2
Les Rousses F	28	C2
Les Sables-d'Olonne F	24	A4
Les Trois-Epis F	23	D2
Les Trois-Moutiers F	18	B1
Les Vans F	33	E1
Lesmont F	21	E3
Lesneven F	8	B2
Lesparre-Médoc F	24	A1
Lessay F	10	A3
Lessines B	5	E1
Lestelle Bétharram F	37	E2
Letmathe D	7	F2
Leucate F	39	E2
Leuglay F	21	E2
Leuk CH	29	E1
Leukerbad CH	29	E1
Leuven (Louvain) B	6	A1
Leuze B	13	E4
Levens F	42	C3
Leverkusen D	7	E1
Levet F	26	B3
Levie F	43	a1
Levier F	28	C3
Levroux F	26	A4
Leyre E	36	C2
Leysdown GB	4	A3
Leysin CH	29	D1
Lezay F	24	C3
Lézignan-Corbières F	39	E3
Lezoux F	26	C1
Libourne F	30	C4
Libramont B	14	B2
Lichtenvoorde NL	7	E3
Liège (Luik) B	14	B4
Lier B	6	A2
Liernais F	27	E4
Liestal CH	29	F3
Lieurey F	11	E2
Liffré F	17	F4
Ligneuville B	14	C3
Lignières F	26	B3
Ligny-en-Barrois F	22	A3
Ligueil F	19	D1
Lille F	5	D1
Lillebonne F	11	E3
Lillers F	4	C1
Limburg D	15	F3
Limoges F	25	E2
Limogne-en-Quercy F	32	A2
Limone Piemonte I	43	D3
Limonest F	34	B4
Limours F	20	A4
Limoux F	39	D2
Lingen D	3	F2
Linz D	15	E3
Lisieux F	11	D2
Lisle F	38	C4
Lisse NL	2	B2
Lit-et-Mixe F	30	A2
Livarot F	11	D2
Livernon F	32	A2
Livron F	34	A2
Lizy F	12	C1
Llançà E	39	E1
Llavorsi E	38	B2
Lles E	38	C1
Lochem NL	7	D3

Loches F.	19	D1
Locmaria F.	16	C3
Locmariaquer F.	16	C3
Locminé F.	17	D4
Locquirec F.	8	C2
Locronan F.	8	B1
Loctudy F.	8	B1
Lodève F.	40	A3
Lodosa E.	36	A2
Loga D.	3	F3
Lohéac F.	17	E4
Lohnsfeld D.	15	F1
Lokeren B.	5	F2
Lombez F.	38	B4
Lomme F.	5	D1
Lommel B.	6	B2
Londinières F.	12	A3
Longeau F.	21	F1
Longny-au-Perche F.	19	D4
Longué F.	18	B2
Longuyon F.	14	B1
Longwy F.	14	B1
Lons-le-Saunier F.	28	B2
Lorcé B.	14	C3
Lorch D.	15	F2
Lorentzen F.	23	D3
Lorgues F.	42	A2
Lorient F.	16	C4
Loriol-sur-Drôme F.	34	A2
Lormes F.	27	E4
Lormont F.	30	C4
Lörrach D.	29	F4
Lorris F.	20	B2
Lorup D.	3	F3
Los Arcos E.	36	A2
Losheim D.	15	D1
Losheim D.	14	C3
Lossburg D.	23	F2
Loudéac F.	9	D1
Loudes F.	33	E3
Loudun F.	18	C1
Loué F.	18	C3
Louhans F.	28	A2
Loulay F.	24	B3
Lourdes F.	37	E2
Louvain (Leuven) B.	6	A1
Louviers F.	11	F2
Lubersac F.	32	A4
Luc-en-Diois F.	34	B1
Luc-sur-Mer F.	10	C3
Lucenay F.	27	E3
Luçon F.	24	B4
Lüdenscheid D.	7	F1
Lüdinghausen D.	7	F2
Ludwigshafen D.	15	F1
Luigny F.	19	E3
Luik (Liège) B.	14	B4
Lumbier E.	36	B2
Lumbres F.	4	C1
Lummen B.	6	B1
Lunas F.	39	F3
Lunel F.	40	B3
Lünen D.	7	F2
Lunéville F.	22	C3
Lungern CH.	29	F2
Lünne D.	3	F1
Lurcy-Lévis F.	26	C3
Lure F.	29	D4
Lureuil F.	25	E3
Lus-la-Croix-Haute F.	34	C1
Lusignan F.	25	D3
Lusigny F.	21	D3
Lussac-les-Châteaux F.	25	E3
Lussan F.	40	C4
Luxembourg L.	14	C2
Luxeuil-les-Bains F.	22	B1
Luz-St-Sauveur F.	37	E2
Luzarches F.	12	B1
Luzy F.	27	E3
Lydd GB.	4	A2
Lympne GB.	4	A2
Lyon F.	34	B4
Lyons-la-Forêt F.	12	A2
Lyss CH.	29	E3

M

Maaseik B.	6	C1
Maasmechelen B.	6	C1
Maassluis NL.	6	A3
Maastricht NL.	6	C1
Machault F.	13	E1
Mâchecourt F.	17	E2
Mâcon F.	27	F2
Made NL.	6	B3
Magescq F.	30	A2
Magnac-Laval F.	25	E2
Magny-en-Vexin F.	12	A2
Maîche F.	29	D3
Maidstone GB.	4	A3
Mailly-le-Camp F.	21	E3
Maintenon F.	19	F4
Mainz D.	15	F2
Malaucène F.	41	D4
Malbuisson F.	28	C2
Maldegem B.	5	E2
Maldon GB.	4	A4
Malesherbes F.	20	B3
Malestroit F.	17	D4
Malicorne F.	18	C3
Malines (Mechelen) B.	6	A1
Malmédy B.	14	C3
Malo-les-Bains F.	4	C2
Mamers F.	19	D4
Mandelieu F.	42	B2
Manderscheid D.	15	D2
Mannheim D.	15	F1
Manosque F.	41	E3
Mansle F.	24	C2
Mantes F.	12	A1
Manzat F.	26	C1
Marans F.	24	B3
Marboz F.	28	A2
Marchaux F.	28	C3
Marche-en-Famenne B.	14	B3
Marcheprime F.	30	B3
Marciac F.	37	E3
Marcigny F.	27	E2
Marcilla E.	36	A1
Marcillac-Vallon F.	32	B2
Marcillat F.	26	B2
Marcilly-le-Hayer F.	21	D3
Marckolsheim F.	23	D2
Marennes F.	24	A2
Mareuil F.	25	D1
Mareuil F.	24	B4
Margate GB.	4	B3
Maria Laach D.	15	E3
Marignane F.	41	D2
Marigny-le-Châtel F.	21	D3
Marines F.	12	B2
Maringues F.	26	C1
Marl D.	7	E2
Marle F.	13	E2
Marlenheim F.	23	D3
Marmande F.	31	D3
Marmoutier F.	23	D3
Marnay F.	28	C3
Marquion F.	13	D3
Marquise F.	4	B2
Marseillan F.	40	A3
Marseillan-Plage F.	40	A3
Marseille F.	41	D2
Marseille-en-Beauvaisis F.	12	B2
Martel F.	32	A3
Martelange B.	14	B2
Martigné-Ferchaud F.	17	F3
Martigny CH.	35	F4
Martigues F.	41	D2
Marvejols F.	33	D2
Marxzell D.	23	F3
Masevaux F.	22	C1
Massat F.	38	B2
Massay F.	26	B4
Masseube F.	38	A4

Massiac F.	33	D3
Matha F.	24	C2
Mathay F.	29	D3
Matignon F.	9	E2
Matour F.	27	E2
Maubeuge F.	13	E3
Maubourguet F.	37	E3
Mauléon F.	18	A1
Mauléon-Licharre F.	36	C3
Maulévrier F.	18	A1
Maupertus-sur-Mer F.	10	B4
Maure F.	17	E4
Mauriac F.	32	C3
Mauron F.	17	E4
Maurs F.	32	B2
Maury F.	39	D2
Mauvezin F.	38	B4
Mauvoisin CH.	35	F4
Mauzé-sur-le-Mignon F.	24	B3
Mayen D.	15	E3
Mayenne F.	18	B4
Mayet F.	18	C3
Mazamet F.	39	D3
Mazères F.	38	C3
Meaux F.	12	C1
Mechelen (Malines) B.	6	A1
Mechernich D.	15	D3
Medemblik NL.	2	C3
Megève F.	35	E4
Mehun-sur-Yèvre F.	26	B4
Meijel NL.	6	C2
Meinerzhagen D.	7	F1
Meiringen CH.	29	F2
Meisenheim D.	15	E1
Mélisey F.	22	C1
Melle F.	24	C3
Melun F.	20	B4
Menat F.	26	C2
Mendavia E.	36	A2
Mende F.	33	D2
Menden D.	7	F2
Menen B.	5	D1
Mens F.	34	C2
Menthon F.	35	D4
Menton F.	42	C3
Meppel NL.	3	D2
Meppen D.	3	F2
Mer F.	19	E2
Merdrignac F.	9	E1
Méréville F.	20	A3
Méribel F.	35	D3
Merligen CH.	29	F2
Mersch L.	14	C2
Mersch D.	7	D1
Méru F.	12	B2
Mervans F.	28	A2
Méry F.	21	D3
Merzig D.	15	D1
Meschers-sur-Gironde F.	24	A2
Meslay F.	18	B3
Mesnil-Val F.	12	A4
Mesvres F.	27	E3
Metabief F.	28	C2
Méteren F.	5	D1
Mettet B.	13	F3
Mettingen D.	7	F3
Mettlach D.	15	D1
Mettmann D.	7	E1
Metz F.	22	C4
Metzervisse F.	14	C1
Meulan F.	12	A1
Meung-sur-Loire F.	19	F2
Meximieux F.	34	B4
Meymac F.	32	B2
Meyrargues F.	41	E3
Meyrueis F.	33	D1
Meyzieu F.	34	B4
Mèze F.	40	A3
Mézel F.	42	A3
Mézières F.	25	E2
Mézières-en-Brenne F.	25	F4
Mézilhac F.	33	F2
Mézin F.	31	D2

Middelburg NL.	5	E3
Middelharnis NL.	6	A3
Middelkerke-Bad B.	5	D2
Midsland NL.	2	C4
Miélan F.	37	F3
Migennes F.	20	C2
Mijoux F.	28	C1
Millas F.	39	D1
Millau F.	32	C1
Mimizan F.	30	A2
Mimizan-Plage F.	30	A2
Mindin F.	17	D2
Minster GB.	4	A3
Miramar F.	42	B2
Miramas F.	41	D3
Mirambeau F.	24	B1
Miramont-de-Guyenne F.	31	D3
Mirande F.	37	F3
Mirebeau F.	25	D4
Mirebeau F.	28	B4
Mirecourt F.	22	B2
Mirepoix F.	38	C3
Modane F.	35	E2
Modave B.	14	B3
Moers D.	7	D2
Moirans F.	34	C3
Moirans-en-Montagne F.	28	B2
Moissac F.	31	E1
Mol B.	6	B2
Molare I.	43	E4
Molières F.	31	F2
Molliens F.	12	B3
Moloy F.	28	A4
Molsheim F.	23	D2
Monaco MC.	42	C2
Moncalieri I.	35	F2
Mönchengladbach D.	7	D1
Moncontour F.	9	D1
Moncoutant F.	24	C4
Mondorf-les-Bains L.	14	C1
Mondoubleau F.	19	D3
Mondovi I.	43	D4
Mondragón E.	36	A3
Monestier-de-Clermont F.	34	C2
Monflanquin F.	31	E2
Monistrol-d'Allier F.	33	E3
Monistrol-sur-Loire F.	33	F3
Monnickendam NL.	2	B2
Monpazier F.	31	E3
Monplaisir F.	19	D3
Monreal E.	36	B2
Mons (Bergen) B.	13	E4
Monschau D.	14	C3
Monségur F.	31	D3
Monsheim D.	15	F1
Mont-de-Marsan F.	30	B2
Mont-Louis F.	38	C1
Mont-sous-Vaudrey F.	28	B3
Montabaur D.	15	F3
Montagnac F.	40	A3
Montaigu F.	17	F2
Montaigu-de-Quercy F.	31	E2
Montaigut F.	26	C2
Montalivet-les-Bains F.	24	A1
Montana CH.	29	E1
Montaren F.	40	C4
Montargis F.	20	B2
Montastruc-la-Conseillère F.	38	C4
Montauban F.	31	F1
Montbard F.	21	D1
Montbazens F.	32	B2
Montbazon F.	19	D2
Montbéliard F.	29	D4
Montbenoît F.	29	D3
Montbonnot F.	34	C2
Montbrison F.	33	F4
Montbron F.	25	D1
Montbrun-les-Bains F.	41	E4
Montceau-les-Mines F.	27	E2
Montcornet F.	13	E2

54

Montcuq F	31	F2	Morteau F	29	D3	Nettancourt F	21	F4	
Montdidier F	12	C2	Mortrée F	11	D1	Nettetal D	7	D2	
Monte-Carlo MC	42	C2	Morzine F	29	D1	Neu-Moresnet B	14	C4	
Montebourg F	10	B3	Mouchard F	28	C3	Neuchâtel CH	29	D3	
Montélimar F	34	A1	Moudon CH	29	D2	Neudorf D	23	F4	
Montendre F	24	B1	Mougins F	42	B2	Neuenburg D	23	D1	
Montereau F	20	B3	Mouliherne F	18	C2	Neuenbürg D	23	F3	
Montesquieu-			Moulins F	27	D2	Neuenhaus D	3	E2	
Volvestre F	38	B3	Moulins-Engilbert F	27	E3	Neuf-Brisach F	23	D1	
Montesquiou F	37	F3	Moulins-la-Marche F	11	D1	Neufchâteau F	22	B2	
Montfaucon-en-Velay F	33	F3	Moustiers-Ste-Marie F	42	A3	Neufchâteau B	14	B2	
Montfort F	30	B1	Mouthe F	28	C2	Neufchâtel F	13	E2	
Montfort F	17	E4	Mouthier F	28	C3	Neufchâtel-en-Bray F	12	A3	
Montfort F	12	A1	Mouthoumet F	39	D2	Neuhausen am			
Montgenèvre F	35	E2	Moutier CH	29	E3	Rheinfall CH	23	F1	
Montgiscard F	38	C3	Moûtiers F	35	D3	Neuillé Port-Pierre F	19	D2	
Montguyon F	31	D4	Moutiers F	24	A4	Neuilly-l'Évêque F	22	A2	
Monthermé F	13	F2	Mouy F	12	B2	Neuilly-St-Front F	13	D1	
Monthey CH	29	D1	Mouzon F	14	A2	Neung-sur-Beuvron F	19	F2	
Monthois F	13	F1	Much D	15	E4	Neunkirchen D	15	D1	
Monthureaux-sur-			Mugron F	30	B1	Neuss D	7	D1	
Saône F	22	B2	Mülheim D	15	D2	Neustadt D	23	E1	
Montier-en-Der F	21	E3	Mülheim D	7	E2	Neustadt an der			
Montignac F	31	F3	Mulhouse F	29	E4	Weinstrasse D	23	F4	
Montigny-le-Roi F	22	A2	Müllheim D	23	D1	Neuves-Maisons F	22	B3	
Montigny-sur-Aube F	21	E2	Münsingen CH	29	D2	Neuvic F	32	C4	
Montivilliers F	11	D3	Münster CH	29	F1	Neuville F	25	D4	
Montlieu-la-Garde F	24	B1	Munster F	23	D2	Neuville-aux-Bois F	20	A3	
Montluçon F	26	B2	Münster D	7	F3	Neuvy F	26	A3	
Montluel F	34	B4	Münstertal D	23	E1	Neuvy-sur-Barangeon F	20	A1	
Montmarault F	26	C2	Mur-de-Barrez F	32	C3	Neuwied D	15	E3	
Montmédy F	14	B2	Mur-de-Bretagne F	9	D1	Nevers F	27	D3	
Montmélian F	35	D3	Murat F	32	C3	New Romney GB	4	A2	
Montmirail F	19	D3	Murat-sur-Vèbre F	39	E3	Nexon F	25	E1	
Montmirail F	21	D4	Murato F	43	b3	Nice F	42	C2	
Montmirey F	28	B3	Muret F	38	B3	Niederbronn-les-			
Montmoreau-			Muro F	43	a3	Bains F	23	E3	
St-Cybard F	24	C1	Mürren CH	29	F1	Niederkrüchten D	7	D1	
Montmorillon F	25	E3	Murten CH	29	E2	Nieppe F	5	D1	
Montmort F	21	D4	Musselkanaal NL	3	F3	Nierstein D	15	F2	
Montoire-sur-le-Loir F	19	D2	Mussidan F	31	D4	Nieuil F	25	D2	
Montpellier F	40	B3	Mussy F	21	E2	Nieuweschans NL	3	E1	
Montpezat F	31	F2	Mutrico E	36	A4	Nieuwpoort B	5	D2	
Montpon-			Mutterstadt D	15	F1	Nijkerk NL	2	C1	
Ménestérol F	31	D4	Muzillac F	17	D3	Nijmegen NL	6	C3	
Montpont-en-Bresse F	28	A2				Nijverdal NL	3	D2	
Montréal F	31	D1				Nîmes F	40	C3	
Montréal F	39	D3				Ninove B	5	F1	
Montréjeau F	37	F2	**N**			Niort F	24	C3	
Montrésor F	19	D1				Nitry F	21	D1	
Montret F	28	A2				Nivelles B	13	F4	
Montreuil F	4	B1				Nizza Monferrato I	43	E4	
Montreuil-aux-Lions F	12	C1	Naarden NL	2	C2	Noailles F	12	B2	
Montreuil-Bellay F	18	B1	Nadrin B	14	B3	Noain E	36	B2	
Montreux CH	29	D1	Nagold D	23	F2	Noeux F	12	C4	
Montrevel F	28	A2	Nailloux F	38	C3	Nogaro F	37	E4	
Montrichard F	19	D2	Najac F	32	A1	Nogent F	21	F2	
Montrond-les-Bains F	33	F4	Nalzen F	38	C2	Nogent-le-Roi F	19	F4	
Monts-s-Guesnes F	18	C1	Namur B	14	A4	Nogent-le-Rotrou F	19	D4	
Montsalvy F	32	C2	Nancy F	22	B3	Nogent-sur-Seine F	20	C3	
Montsauche-les-			Nangis F	20	C3	Nohfelden D	15	D1	
Settons F	27	E4	Nans-les-Pins F	41	E2	Noirétable F	33	E4	
Montsoreau F	18	C2	Nant F	40	A4	Noirmoutier-en-l'Ile F	17	D2	
Montsûrs F	18	B4	Nantes F	17	E2	Nolay F	27	F3	
Moordorf D	3	F4	Nanteuil-le-Haudouin F	12	C1	Nomeny F	22	C3	
Morbach D	15	D2	Nantiat F	25	E2	Nomexy F	22	C2	
Morcenx F	30	B2	Nantua F	28	B1	Nonancourt F	11	E1	
Mordelles F	17	E4	Narbonne F	39	E2	Nonant-le-Pin F	11	D1	
Morestel F	34	C3	Narbonne-Plage F	39	E2	Nontron F	25	D1	
Moretta I	35	F1	Nasbinals F	33	D2	Nonza F	43	b3	
Moreuil F	12	C3	Nassau D	15	F3	Noordwijk aan Zee NL	2	A2	
Morez F	28	C2	Navarrenx F	37	D3	Nordausques F	4	C2	
Morgat F	8	B2	Navilly F	28	A3	Norddeich D	3	F4	
Morges CH	29	D2	Neauvic F	31	E4	Norden D	3	F4	
Morgex F	35	E3	Neede NL	7	E3	Norderney D	3	F4	
Morgins CH	29	D1	Neermoor D	3	F3	Nordhorn D	3	E2	
Morhange F	22	C3	Neheim-Hüsten D	7	F2	Norg NL	3	E3	
Morlaàs F	37	E3	Nemours F	20	B3	Nort F	17	F3	
Morlaix F	8	C2	Nérac F	31	D2	Nottuln D	7	F3	
Mormant F	20	B4	Néris-les-Bains F	26	B2	Nouan-le-Fuzelier F	19	F2	
Morosaglia F	43	b2	Nérondes F	26	C3	Nouans-les-Fontaines F	19	E1	
Mortagne-au-Perche F	19	D4	Nervi I	43	F4	Nouvion F	12	B4	
Mortagne-sur-Sèvre F	17	F1	Nes NL	3	D4	Noves F	41	D3	
Mortain F	10	B1	Nesle F	12	C3	Novi Ligure I	43	F4	
						Novion-Porcien F	13	F2	
						Noyant F	18	C2	
						Noyers F	21	D1	
						Noyers-sur-Jabron F	41	F4	
						Noyon F	12	C2	
						Nozay F	17	E3	

DIEPPE

ROUEN

Vigny — Ableiges

La Villeneuve-
St-Martin — N14 — Osr

D28

CE
PON

Meulan — D190

Les
Mureaux — Triel-
sur-Seine

EVREUX ROUEN — Vernouillet — 8

Carrières-
sous-Pois

D113 — S

Orgeval — ST-C
E

Crespières — D30 — A13
E05

D307 — D5

St-Nom-
la-Bretèche — D98

Les Clayes-
sous-Bois

ALENÇON — N12

Trappes — N10 — Monti
le Bretô

Maurepas

CHARTRES — Le Mesnil-
St-Denis

Nizza — St
les-C

Les-Essarts-
le-Roi — D91

Chevreuse

Cernay-
la-Ville

D906

Parc Naturel
Régional de
la Haute Vallée
de Chevreuse — D24

Bonnelles

CHARTRES

Oisterwijk NL — 6 B2
Olargues F — 39 E3
Olazagutía E — 36 A3
Oldenzaal NL — 7 E4
Oletta F — 43 b3
Olette F — 39 D1
Olite E — 36 B2
Olivet F — 19 F2
Olliergues F — 33 E4
Olmeto F — 43 a1
Olonzac F — 39 E3
Oloron-Ste-Marie F — 37 D3
Olpe D — 15 F4
Olst NL — 3 D2
Olten CH — 29 F3
Ommen NL — 3 D2
Onnaing F — 13 E4
Oostburg NL — 5 E2
Oostende B — 5 D2
Oosterbeek NL — 6 C3
Oostérend NL — 2 C4
Oosterhout NL — 6 B3
Oosterwolde NL — 3 D3
Oostmalle B — 6 B2
Ootmarsum NL — 3 E2
Opladen D — 7 E1
Oppenau D — 23 E2
Oppenheim D — 15 F2
Oraison F — 41 F3
Orange F — 41 D4
Orbassano I — 35 F2
Orbe CH — 29 D2
Orbec F — 11 D2
Orbey F — 23 D2
Orchies F — 13 D4
Orcières F — 35 D1
Ordino AND — 38 B2
Orford GB — 4 B4
Orgelet F — 28 B2
Orgeval F — 12 A1
Orgon F — 41 D3
Orio E — 36 A3
Orléans F — 19 F2
Orly F — 20 B4
Ornans F — 28 C3
Oron-la-Ville CH — 29 D2
Orscholz D — 14 C1
Orsières CH — 35 F4
Orthez F — 37 D3
Ospedaletti I — 43 D3
Oss NL — 6 C3
Ostbevern D — 7 F3
Osthofen D — 15 F1
Ostiz E — 36 B3
Otterbach D — 15 E1
Otterlo NL — 6 C3
Ottweiler D — 15 D1
Oucques F — 19 E2
Oud Beijerland NL — 6 A3
Ouddorp NL — 5 F3
Oude-Pekela NL — 3 F3
Oudenaarde B — 5 E1
Ouistreham F — 10 C3
Oulx I — 35 E2
Oust F — 38 B2
Ouzouer-le-Marché F — 19 E3
Ovada I — 43 E4
Overath D — 15 E4
Oyonnax F — 28 B1

P

Pacy-sur-Eure F — 11 F1
Paesana I — 35 E1
Pagny F — 22 B4
Paimboeuf F — 17 E2
Paimpol F — 9 D2
Paladru F — 34 C3
Palavas-les-Flots F — 40 B3
Paliseul B — 14 A2

Pamiers F — 38 C3
Pamplona/Iruñea E — 36 B2
Panassac F — 38 A4
Papenburg D — 3 F3
Paray-le-Monial F — 27 E2
Parentis-en-Born F — 30 B3
Paris F — 12 B1
Parkeston Quay GB — 4 B4
Parthenay F — 24 C4
Partinello F — 43 a2
Pas de la Casa AND — 38 C1
Pas-en-Artois F — 12 C4
Pasaia E — 36 B3
Patay F — 19 F3
Pau F — 37 D3
Pauillac F — 24 B1
Paulhaguet F — 33 E3
Pavilly F — 11 E3
Payerne CH — 29 D2
Payrac F — 32 A3
Péaule F — 17 D3
Pegli I — 43 F4
Peira-Cava I — 42 C3
Pellegrue F — 31 D3
Pentrez-Plage F — 8 B2
Peralta E — 36 A1
Percy F — 10 B2
Périers F — 10 B3
Perkpolder NL — 5 F2
Pernes F — 41 D4
Péronne F — 12 C3
Pérouges F — 34 B4
Perpignan F — 39 E1
Perros-Guirec F — 9 D3
Pertuis F — 41 E3
Péruwelz B — 13 E4
Pesmes F — 28 B3
Petange L — 14 B1
Petreto-Bicchisano F — 43 a1
Peyrat-le-Château F — 25 F1
Peyrehorade F — 36 C4
Peyrolles F — 41 E3
Peyruis F — 41 F3
Pézenas F — 40 A3
Pforzheim D — 23 F3
Phalsbourg F — 23 D3
Philippeville B — 13 F3
Piana F — 43 a2
Piana Crixia I — 43 E4
Picquigny F — 12 B3
Piedicroce F — 43 b2
Pierre-Buffière F — 25 E1
Pierre-de-Bresse F — 28 B3
Pierrefitte F — 22 A4
Pierrefitte-Nestalas F — 37 E2
Pierrefonds F — 12 C2
Pierrefort F — 32 C3
Pierrelatte F — 34 A1
Pierroton F — 30 B3
Pilat-Plage F — 30 B3
Pinerolo I — 35 F1
PineУ F — 21 E3
Pino F — 43 b3
Pinols F — 33 D3
Pionsat F — 26 B2
Pipriac F — 17 E3
Piriac-sur-Mer F — 17 D3
Pirmasens D — 23 E4
Pirou-Plage F — 10 A3
Pissos F — 30 B3
Pithiviers F — 20 A3
Plabennec F — 8 B2
Plaisance F — 37 E3
Plancoët F — 9 E2
Pleaux F — 32 B3
Plélan-le-Grand F — 17 E4
Plestin-les-Grèves F — 8 C2
Plettenberg D — 7 F1
Pleumartin F — 25 E4
Pleyben F — 8 B2
Ploërmel F — 17 D4
Plombières-les-Bains F — 22 C2
Plonéour Lanvern F — 8 B1

Plouaret F — 8 C2
Plouay F — 16 C4
Ploubalay F — 9 E2
Ploudalmézeau F — 8 B3
Plouescat F — 8 B3
Plougasnou F — 8 C2
Plouguenast F — 9 D1
Plouha F — 9 D2
Plouigneau F — 8 C2
Plouray F — 8 C1
Plozévet F — 8 B1
Pluvigner F — 16 C4
Podensac F — 30 C3
Poeldijk NL — 6 A4
Poissons F — 21 F3
Poitiers F — 25 D3
Poix F — 12 B3
Poix-Terron F — 13 F2
Poligny F — 28 B2
Pompaples CH — 29 D2
Pompey F — 22 B3
Poncin F — 28 B1
Pons F — 24 B2
Pont-Audemer F — 11 E2
Pont-Aven F — 8 B1
Pont-à-Mousson F — 22 B4
Pont-Croix F — 8 A1
Pont-d'Ain F — 28 A1
Pont-de-Briques F — 4 B1
Pont-de-Dore F — 27 D1
Pont-de-l'Arche F — 11 F2
Pont-de-Roide F — 29 D3
Pont-de-Salars F — 32 C1
Pont-de-Vaux F — 28 A2
Pont-en-Royans F — 34 B2
Pont-l'Abbé F — 8 B1
Pont-l'Evêque F — 11 D2
Pont-Réan F — 17 E4
Pont-Scorff F — 16 C4
Pont-St-Esprit F — 41 D4
Pont-St-Vincent F — 22 B3
Pont-sur-Yonne F — 20 C3
Pontacq F — 37 E3
Pontailler-sur-Saône F — 28 B3
Pontarion F — 26 A2
Pontarlier F — 28 C2
Pontaubault F — 10 A2
Pontaumur F — 26 B1
Pontcharra F — 35 D3
Pontchartrain F — 12 A1
Pontchâteau F — 17 E3
Ponte-Leccia F — 43 b2
Pontgibaud F — 26 C1
Pontigny F — 20 C2
Pontivy F — 9 D1
Pontlevoy F — 19 E2
Pontoise F — 12 B1
Pontorson F — 10 A1
Pontrieux F — 9 D2
Pontvallain F — 18 C3
Poperinge B — 5 D1
Pornic F — 17 D2
Pornichet F — 17 D3
Porquerolles F — 41 F1
Porrentruy CH — 29 E3
Port-Barcarès F — 39 E2
Port-Camargue F — 40 B3
Port-Cros F — 42 A1
Port-de-Bouc F — 41 D2
Port-en-Bessin F — 10 C3
Port-Grimaud F — 42 B2
Port-Leucate F — 39 E2
Port-Louis F — 16 C4
Port-la-Nouvelle F — 39 E2
Port-Manech F — 16 B4
Port-Navalo F — 16 C3
Port-St-Louis-du-
Rhône F — 40 C2
Port-Ste-Marie F — 31 D2
Port-sur-Saône F — 22 B1
Port-Vendres F — 39 E1
Portbail F — 10 A3
Portbou E — 39 E1
Porticcio F — 43 a2

Porto F — 43 a2
Porto-Vecchio F — 43 b1
Portofino I — 43 F3
Pouancé F — 18 A3
Pougues-les-Eaux F — 26 C4
Pouilly F — 26 C4
Pouilly-en-Auxois F — 27 F4
Pouyastruc F — 37 E3
Pouzauges F — 18 A1
Pradelles F — 33 E2
Prades F — 39 D1
Prahecq F — 24 C3
Pralognan-la-Vanoise F — 35 E3
Prats-de-Mollo-la-
Preste F — 39 D1
Prauthoy F — 21 F1
Pré St-Didier I — 35 E3
Pré-en-Pail F — 10 C1
Précy-sous-Thil F — 27 F4
Prémery F — 27 D4
Pressac F — 25 D2
Preuilly-sur-Claise F — 25 E4
Primel-Trégastel F — 8 C3
Primstal D — 15 D1
Privas F — 34 A2
Profondeville B — 14 A3
Pronsfeld D — 14 C3
Propriano F — 43 a1
Provins F — 20 C3
Prüm D — 15 D3
Prunete F — 43 b2
Puente la Reina E — 36 B2
Puffendorf D — 7 D1
Puget-sur-Argens F — 42 B2
Puget-Théniers F — 42 B3
Puget-Ville F — 41 F2
Puigcerda F — 38 C1
Puiseaux F — 20 B3
Puivert F — 38 C2
Purmerend NL — 2 B2
Putanges-Pont-Ecrepin F — 10 C1
Puttelange F — 23 D4
Putten NL — 2 C1
Puy de Dôme F — 26 C1
Puy-Guillaume F — 27 D1
Puy-l'Evêque F — 31 E2
Puylaurens F — 39 D3
Pyla-sur-Mer F — 30 B3

Q

Quarré-les-Tombes F — 27 E4
Questembert F — 17 D3
Quettehou F — 10 B3
Quiberon F — 16 C3
Quillan F — 39 D2
Quimper F — 8 B1
Quimperlé F — 16 C4
Quinéville F — 10 B3
Quingey F — 28 C3
Quintin F — 9 D2
Quissac F — 40 B4

R

Raalte NL — 3 D2
Rabastens F — 38 C4
Rabastens-de-Bigorre F — 37 E3
Racconigi I — 35 F1
Radevormwald D — 7 E1
Raesfeld D — 7 E2
Rambervillers F — 22 C2
Rambouillet F — 19 F4
Ramsgate GB — 4 B3
Ramstein D — 15 E1
Randan F — 26 C1

Rânes F.	10	C1
Raon-l'Etape F.	22	C2
Raron CH	29	F1
Rastatt D.	23	F3
Ratingen D.	7	E2
Raversijde B	5	D2
Rayleigh GB	4	A4
Rayol F.	42	A1
Réalmont F.	39	D4
Rebais F.	20	C4
Recey-sur-Ource F.	21	E1
Recke D.	7	F4
Recklinghausen D	7	E2
Recologne F.	28	C3
Redon F.	17	E3
Rees D.	7	D3
Reignier F.	28	C1
Reims F.	13	E1
Reinach CH	29	F3
Reinsfeld D.	15	D2
Reken D.	7	E3
Remagen D.	15	E3
Rémalard F.	19	D4
Remich L.	14	C1
Remiremont F.	22	C2
Remouchamps B.	14	C3
Remoulins F.	40	C4
Remscheid D	7	E1
Rémuzat F.	34	B1
Renaison F.	27	D1
Renaix (Ronse) B.	5	E1
Renchen D.	23	E3
Renkum NL.	6	C3
Rennerod D.	15	F3
Rennes F.	17	F4
Renteria E.	36	B3
Réquista F.	32	B1
Ressons F.	12	C2
Rethel F.	13	E2
Retiers F.	17	F3
Retournac F.	33	E3
Reuilly F.	26	B4
Reusel NL.	6	B2
Revel F.	39	D3
Révigny F.	21	F4
Revin F.	13	F3
Rhede D.	7	E3
Rheinau D.	23	E3
Rheinbach D	15	D3
Rheinberg D.	7	D2
Rheinböllen D.	15	E2
Rheindahlen D.	7	D1
Rheine D.	7	F3
Rheinfelden CH	29	F4
Rheinfelden D.	29	F4
Rheinzabern D.	23	F4
Rhenen NL.	6	C3
Rhens D.	15	E3
Rheydt D.	7	D1
Rhinau F.	23	E2
Rhynern D.	7	F2
Riaillé F.	17	F3
Rians F.	41	E3
Ribeauville F.	23	D2
Ribécourt F.	12	C2
Ribemont F.	13	D3
Ribérac F.	31	E4
Ribes de Freser E.	38	C1
Richelieu F.	18	C1
Riegel D.	23	E2
Rieumes F.	38	B3
Rieupeyroux F.	32	B2
Rieux F.	38	B3
Riez F.	41	F3
Rignac F.	32	B2
Rijssen NL.	3	E1
Rille F.	18	C2
Riom F.	26	C1
Riom-ès-Montagnes F.	32	C3
Rioz F.	28	C4
Ripoll E.	38	C1
Riquewihr F.	23	D2
Riscle F.	37	E3
Riva-Bella F.	10	C3

Rivarolo Canavese I	35	F2
Rive-de-Gier F.	34	A3
Rivesaltes F.	39	E2
Rivoli I.	35	F2
Roanne F.	27	E1
Rocamadour F.	32	A3
Rochechouart F.	25	D2
Rochefort F.	24	B2
Rochefort B.	14	B3
Rochefort-en-Terre F.	17	D3
Rochefort-s-Nenon F.	28	B3
Rochehaut B.	14	A2
Rochemaure F.	34	A1
Rocheservière F.	17	E2
Rochester GB.	4	A3
Rockenhausen D.	15	E1
Rocroi F.	13	F3
Roden NL.	3	E3
Rodez F.	32	C2
Roermond NL.	6	C1
Roeselare (Roulers) B.	5	D2
Rogliano I.	43	b3
Rognac F.	41	D2
Rohan F.	9	D1
Rohrbach-lès-Bitche F.	23	D4
Roisel F.	13	D3
Rolle CH.	28	C2
Romans-sur-Isère F.	34	B2
Rombas F.	22	B4
Romilly-sur-Seine F.	21	D3
Romont F.	29	D2
Romorantin-Lanthenay F.	19	E1
Roncal E.	36	C2
Roncesvalles E.	36	C3
Ronchamp F.	29	D4
Ronse (Renaix) B.	5	E1
Roodeschool NL.	3	E4
Roosendaal NL.	6	A2
Roquebillière F.	42	C3
Roquebrune-Cap-		
Martin F.	42	C3
Roquefort F.	30	C2
Roquefort-sur-Soulzon F.	39	F4
Rosans F.	34	B1
Roscoff F.	8	C3
Rosporden F.	8	B1
Rostassac F.	31	F2
Rostrenen F.	8	C1
Rothéneuf F.	9	F2
Rotterdam NL.	6	A3
Rottweil D.	23	F2
Roubaix F.	5	D1
Rouen F.	11	F2
Rouffach F.	23	D1
Rougé F.	17	F3
Rougemont F.	29	D4
Rougemont F.	29	E4
Rouillac F.	24	C2
Roujan F.	39	F3
Roulers (Roeselare) B.	5	D2
Roussillon F.	41	D3
Rouvres-en-Xaintois F.	22	B2
Royan F.	24	A2
Royat F.	26	C1
Roybon F.	34	B3
Roye F.	12	C3
Royère-de-Vassivière F.	26	A1
Rozay-en-Brie F.	20	C4
Rozoy F.	13	E2
Rüdesheim D.	15	F2
Rue F.	12	B4
Ruelle-sur-Touvre F.	24	C2
Ruffec F.	25	D2
Ruffieux F.	34	C4
Rugles F.	11	E1
Rülzheim D.	23	F4
Rumigny F.	13	E2
Rumilly F.	35	D4
Rupt F.	22	C1
Rust D.	23	E2
Ruswil CH.	29	F2
Rutenbrock D.	3	F2
Ruurlo NL.	7	D3
Ruwer D.	15	D2

Rye GB.	4	A2
Rysum D.	3	F4

S

Saales F.	23	D2
Saanen CH.	29	E1
Saarbrücken D.	23	D4
Saarburg D.	15	D1
Saarlouis D.	15	D1
Sabiñánigo E.	37	D1
Sablé-sur-Sarthe F.	18	B3
Sables-d'Or-les-Pins F.	9	E2
Sabres F.	30	B2
Sadaba E.	36	B1
Saerbeck D.	7	F3
Saeul L.	14	C2
Sagone F.	43	a2
Saignelégier CH.	29	E3
Saillagouse F.	38	C1
Saillans F.	34	B2
Sains F.	13	D3
St-Affrique F.	39	E4
St-Agnant F.	24	B2
St-Agrève F.	33	F2
St-Aignan F.	18	A3
St-Aignan F.	19	E1
St-Alban F.	33	D2
St-Amand-en-Puisaye F.	20	B1
St-Amand-Longpré F.	19	D2
St-Amand-les-Eaux F.	13	D4
St-Amand-Montrond F.	26	B3
St-Amans F.	33	D2
St-Amant-Roche-		
Savine F.	33	E4
St-Ambroix F.	33	E1
St-Amé F.	22	C2
St-Amour F.	28	B2
St-André F.	11	F1
St-André-de-Cubzac F.	30	C4
St-André-les-Alpes F.	42	B3
St Annaparochie NL.	3	D4
St-Anthème F.	33	E4
St-Antonin-Noble-Val F.	32	A1
St-Aubin-d'Aubigné F.	9	F1
St-Aubin-du-Cormier F.	17	F4
St-Aubin-sur-Mer F.	10	C3
St-Aulaye F.	31	D4
St-Avold F.	22	C4
St-Aygulf F.	42	B2
St-Bard F.	26	B1
St-Béat F.	38	A3
St-Beauzély F.	32	C1
St-Benin F.	27	D3
St-Benoît F.	25	F3
St-Benoît-sur-Loire F.	20	A2
St-Bertrand-de-		
Comminges F.	37	F2
St Blasien D.	23	E1
St-Blin F.	22	A2
St-Bonnet F.	34	C1
St-Bonnet-de-Joux F.	27	E2
St-Bonnet-le-Château F.	33	F3
St-Brevin-les-Pins F.	17	D2
St-Brice-en-Coglès F.	10	A1
St-Brieuc F.	9	D2
St-Calais F.	19	D3
St-Cast-le-Guildo F.	9	E2
St-Céré F.	32	B3
St-Cergue CH.	28	C2
St-Cernin F.	32	C3
St-Chamas F.	41	D3
St-Chély-d'Apcher F.	33	D2
St-Chély-d'Aubrac F.	32	C2
St-Chinian F.	39	E3
St-Ciers F.	24	B1
St-Claud F.	25	D1
St-Claude F.	28	B1

St-Cyprien F.	31	F3
St-Cyprien-Plage F.	39	E1
St-Denis F.	12	B1
St-Denis d'Orques F.	18	B3
St-Denis-d'Oléron F.	24	A3
St-Didier-en-Velay F.	33	F3
St-Dié F.	23	D2
St-Dizier F.	21	F3
St-Donat-sur-l		
'Herbasse F.	34	B2
St-Emilion F.	31	D3
St-Étienne F.	41	E3
St-Étienne F.	33	F3
St-Étienne-de-Baïgorry F.	36	C3
St-Étienne-de-		
St-Geoirs F.	34	B3
St-Étienne-de-Tinée F.	42	B4
St-Fargeau F.	20	B2
St-Firmin F.	34	C2
St-Florent F.	43	b3
St-Florent F.	18	A2
St-Florent F.	26	B4
St-Florentin F.	21	D2
St-Flour F.	33	D3
St-Fulgent F.	17	F1
St-Galmier F.	33	F4
St-Gaudens F.	38	A3
St-Gaultier F.	25	F3
St-Geniez-d'Olt F.	32	C2
St-Genis-de-Saintonge F.	24	B1
St-Genix-sur-Guiers F.	34	C3
St Georgen D.	23	F1
St-Georges F.	18	A2
St-Georges-de-		
Didonne F.	24	A2
St-Geours-de-		
Maremne F.	30	A1
St-Germain F.	25	E1
St-Germain F.	12	B1
St-Germain-de-Joux F.	28	B1
St-Germain-des-Vaux F.	10	A4
St-Germain-du-Bois F.	28	B2
St-Germain-du-Plain F.	28	A2
St-Germain-Laval F.	33	F4
St-Germain-Lembron F.	33	D4
St-Germain-l'Herm F.	33	E4
St-Germain-Plage F.	10	A3
St-Gervais F.	39	E3
St-Gervais-d'Auvergne F.	26	C1
St-Gervais-les-Bains F.	35	E4
St-Géry F.	32	A2
St-Gildas-des-Bois F.	17	E3
St-Gilles F.	40	C3
St-Gilles-Croix-de-Vie F.	17	D1
St Gingolph CH.	29	D1
St-Girons F.	38	B3
St-Girons-Plage F.	30	A2
St Goar D.	15	E2
St Goarshausen D.	15	E2
St-Gorgon-Main F.	28	C3
St-Guénolé F.	8	A1
St-Helier GBJ.	9	F3
St-Hilaire-de-		
Villefranche F.	24	B2
St-Hilaire-du-Harcouët F.	10	B1
St-Hippolyte F.	29	D3
St-Hippolyte-du-Fort F.	40	B4
St-Honoré F.	27	E3
St-Hubert B.	14	B3
St-Imier CH.	29	E3
St Ingbert D.	23	D4
St-Jacut F.	9	E2
St-James F.	10	A1
St-Jean-Brévelay F.	17	D4
St-Jean-Cap-Ferrat F.	42	C2
St-Jean-d'Angély F.	24	B2
St-Jean-de-Bournay F.	34	B3
St-Jean-de-Losne F.	28	B3
St-Jean-de-Luz F.	36	B3
St-Jean-de-Maurienne F.	35	D2
St-Jean-de-Monts F.	17	D1
St-Jean-du-Bruel F.	40	A4
St-Jean-du-Gard F.	40	B4
St-Jean-le-Thomas F.	10	A2

57

St-Jean-Pied-de-Port F 36 C3
St-Jeoire F 28 C1
St-Jorioz F 35 D4
St-Jory F 38 C4
St-Jouan-de-l'Isle F 9 E1
St-Julien F 38 B3
St-Julien-Chapteuil F 33 E3
St-Julien-de-Vouvantes F ... 17 F3
St-Julien-en-Beauchêne F... 34 C1
St-Julien-en-Genevois F..... 28 C1
St-Julien-l'Ars F 25 D3
St-Junien F 25 E2
St-Just-en-Chaussée F 12 B2
St-Just-en-Chevalet F 27 D1
St-Justin F 30 C2
St-Lary-Soulan F 37 E2
St-Laurent F 25 E2
St-Laurent F 10 C3
St-Laurent-en-
    Grandvaux F 28 C2
St-Laurent-Médoc F 24 A1
St-Leger F 27 E3
St-Léonard-de-Noblat F....... 25 F1
St-Lô F 10 B2
St-Louis F 29 F4
St-Loup-sur-Semouse F....... 22 B1
St-Luc CH 29 E1
St-Lunaire F 9 E2
St-Lys F 38 B4
St-Macaire F 30 C3
St-Maclou F 11 D2
St-Maixent-l'Ecole F 24 C3
St-Malo F 9 F2
St-Marcellin F 34 B2
St Märgen D 23 E1
St-Mars-la-Jaille F 17 F3
St-Martin-d'Auxigny F 26 B4
St-Martin-de-Londres F...... 40 B3
St-Martin-de-Ré F 24 A3
St-Martin-Vésubie F 42 C3
St-Martory F 38 B3
St-Mathieu F 25 D1
St-Maurice CH 29 D1
St Maurice-sur-Moselle F... 22 C1
St-Maximin-la-Ste-
    Baume F 41 E2
St-Méen F 9 E1
St-Michel-de-
    Maurienne F 35 D2
St-Michel-en-Grève F 8 C2
St-Michel-en-l'Herm F 24 A3
St-Mihiel F 22 A4
St-Nazaire F 17 D2
St-Nectaire F 33 D4
St-Nicolas F 17 E3
St Nicolas-de-Port F 22 C3
St-Nicolas-du-Pélem F....... 9 D2
St-Niklaas B 5 F2
St Niklaus CH 29 F1
St Oedenrode NL 6 C2
St-Omer F 4 C1
St-Palais F 36 C3
St-Palais-sur-Mer F 24 A2
St-Pardoux-la-Rivière F...... 25 D1
St-Paul F 42 C2
St-Paul F 35 D1
St-Paul-Cap-de-Joux F 39 D4
St-Paul-de-Fenouillet F...... 39 D2
St-Pauliene F 33 E3
St-Pé F 37 E2
St-Péray F 34 A2
St-Père-en-Retz F 17 E2
St-Peter Port GBG 9 E4
St-Philbert F 17 E2
St-Pierre-d'Albigny F 35 D3
St-Pierre-d'Oléron F 24 A3
St-Pierre-de-
    Chartreuse F 34 C3
St-Pierre-de-Chignac F...... 31 E4
St-Pierre-Église F 10 B4
St-Pierre-le-Moûtier F 26 C3
St-Pierre-Quiberon F 16 C3
St-Pierre-sur-Dives F......... 11 D2
St-Pois F 10 B2

St-Pol-de-Léon F 8 C3
St-Pol-sur-Ternoise F......... 12 C4
St-Pons F 39 E3
St-Porchaire F 24 B2
St-Pourçain F 26 C2
St-Privat F 32 B3
St-Quay-Portrieux F 9 D2
St-Quentin F 13 D3
St-Rambert-d'Albon F......... 34 A3
St-Rambert-en-Bugey F...... 34 C4
St-Raphaël F 42 B2
St-Rémy-de-Provence F...... 41 D3
St-Renan F 8 A2
St-Riquier F 12 B4
St-Rome-de-Tarn F 39 E4
St-Saëns F 11 F3
St-Satur F 20 B1
St-Saulge F 27 D4
St-Sauvant F 25 D3
St-Sauveur-en-Puisaye F.... 20 B2
St-Sauveur-le-Vicomte F.... 10 B3
St-Sauveur-sur-Tinée F...... 42 C3
St-Savin F 30 C4
St-Savin F 25 E3
St-Seine-l'Abbaye F 28 A4
St-Sernin-sur-Rance F 39 E4
St-Sever F 30 B1
St-Sever F 10 B2
St-Symphorien F 30 C3
St-Symphorien-d'Ozon F... 34 B4
St-Symphorien-de-Lay F.... 27 E1
St-Symphorien-sur-
    Coise F 34 A4
St-Thiébault F 22 A2
St-Trivier-de-Courtes F...... 28 A2
St-Tropez F 42 B2
St-Truiden B 6 B1
St-Vaast-la-Hougue F 10 B3
St-Valery-en-Caux F 11 E3
St-Valery-sur-Somme F...... 12 B4
St-Vallier-de-Thiey F 42 B3
St-Vallier-sur-Rhône F....... 34 A3
St-Vaury F 26 A2
St-Véran F 35 E1
St Vincent I 35 F3
St-Vincent-de-Tyrosse F.... 30 A1
St Vith B 14 C3
St-Vivien-de-Médoc F 24 A1
St Wendel D 15 D1
St-Yrieix-la-Perche F 25 E1
Ste-Anne-d'Auray F 16 C4
Ste-Anne-la-Palud F 8 B2
Ste-Croix CH 29 D2
Ste-Croix-Volvestre F 38 B3
Ste-Enimie F 33 D1
Ste-Foy-la-Grande F 31 D3
Ste-Gauburge-Ste-
    Colombe F 11 D1
Ste-Hélène F 30 B4
Ste-Hermine F 24 B4
Ste-Marie-aux-Mines F...... 23 D2
Ste-Marie-de-Campan F.... 37 E2
Ste-Maure-de-Touraine F... 18 C1
Ste-Maxime F 42 B2
Ste-Menehould F 21 F4
Ste-Mère-Eglise F 10 B3
Ste-Sévère F 26 B3
Ste-Suzanne F 18 B3
Ste-Tulle F 41 E3
Stes-Maries-de-la-Mer F.... 40 C3
Sainte-Lucie-de-Tallano F... 43 a1
Sainte-Marie-Sicché F....... 43 a2
Saintes F 24 B2
Saissac F 39 D3
Sallardú E 38 A2
Salbris F 19 F1
Salernes F 42 A2
Salers F 32 C3
Salies-de-Béarn F 37 D3
Salies-du-Salat F 38 B3
Salignac-Eyvigues F 31 F3
Salins F 28 C3
Sallanches F 35 E4
Sallent de Gállego E 37 D2

Salles F 30 B3
Salles F 38 C3
Salles-Curan F 32 C1
Salon F 21 D3
Salon-de-Provence F 41 D3
Salses-le-Château F 39 E2
Saluzzo I 35 F1
Salvatierra E 36 A3
Salviac F 31 F3
Samadet F 37 D4
Samatan F 38 B4
Samer F 4 B1
Samitier E 37 E1
Samoëns F 35 E4
San Anton Leitza E 36 B3
San Martín de Unx E 36 B2
San Remo I 43 D3
San Sebastián/
    Donostia E 36 B3
Sanary-sur-Mer F 41 E2
Sancergues F 26 C4
Sancerre F 20 B1
Sancoins F 26 C3
Sandgate GB 4 A2
Sandwich GB 4 B3
Sangüesa E 36 B2
Sanguinet F 30 B3
Sannenmöser CH 29 E1
Sant Julià de Lória AND..... 38 B1
Sant Kurutze Kampezu E.. 36 A2
Santa Joan de les
    Abadesses E 39 D1
Santa Margherita
    Ligure I 43 F3
Santa Severa I 43 b3
Santena I 35 F2
Santesteban E 36 B3
Sappemeer NL 3 E3
Saqués E 37 D2
Saramon F 38 B4
Sarlat-la-Canéda F 31 F3
Sarralbe F 23 D4
Sarre-Union F 23 D3
Sarrebourg F 23 D3
Sarreguemines F 23 D4
Sarron F 37 E3
Sartène F 43 a1
Sartilly F 10 A2
Sarzeau F 17 D3
Sassenage F 34 C2
Sassenheim NL 2 B2
Saucats F 30 C3
Saugues F 33 D3
Saujon F 24 B2
Saulieu F 27 E4
Sault F 41 E4
Saulx F 22 B1
Saulxures F 22 C1
Saumur F 18 B2
Sauve F 40 B4
Sauveterre-de-Béarn F...... 36 C3
Sauveterre-de-
    Guyenne F 31 D3
Sauxillanges F 33 D4
Sauze d'Oulx I 35 E2
Sauzé-Vaussais F 24 C2
Sauzon F 16 C3
Savenay F 17 E3
Saverdun F 38 C3
Saverne F 23 D3
Savigliano I 35 F1
Savignac-les-Eglises F....... 31 F4
Savigny-sur-Braye F 19 D3
Savines-le-Lac F 35 D1
Scaër F 8 C1
Schaffhausen CH 23 F1
Schagen NL 2 B3
Schermbeck D 7 E2
Scheveningen NL 2 A1
Schiermonnikoog NL 3 D4
Schifferstadt D 23 F4
Schilde B 6 A2
Schiltach D 23 F2

Schirmeck F 23 D2
Schlangenbad D 15 F2
Schleiden D 15 D3
Schluchsee D 23 E1
Schönau D 29 F4
Schönecken D 15 D3
Schönwald D 23 E1
Schoondijke NL 5 E2
Schoonebeek NL 3 E2
Schoonhoven NL 6 B3
Schoonoord NL 3 E2
Schopfheim D 29 F4
Schramberg D 23 F2
Schüpfheim CH 29 F2
Schüttorf D 7 F4
Schwarzsee CH 29 E2
Schweich D 15 D2
Schwelm D 7 E1
Schwenningen D 23 F1
Schwerte D 7 E1
Schwetzingen D 23 F4
Seclin F 13 D4
Secondigny F 24 C4
Sedan F 14 A2
Séderon F 41 E4
Seelbach D 23 E2
Sées F 11 D1
Segonzac F 24 C2
Segré F 18 A3
Seiches-sur-le-Loir F 18 B2
Seilhac F 32 B4
Seira E 37 E1
Sélestat F 23 D2
Selles F 19 E1
Sellières F 28 B2
Selm D 7 F2
Selongey F 21 F1
Seltz F 23 E3
Semur-en-Auxois F 21 D1
Sénas F 41 D3
Senden D 7 F3
Sendenhorst D 7 F2
Senlis F 12 B2
Sennecey-le-Grand F 28 A2
Senonches F 19 E4
Senones F 23 D2
Sens F 20 C3
Sept-Saulx F 13 E1
Seraing B 14 B4
Sérent F 17 D4
Sermaize-les-Bains F 21 F3
Serres F 34 C1
Serrières F 34 A3
Sesma E 36 A2
Sestriere I 35 E2
Sète F 40 B3
Settimo Torinese I 35 F2
Seurre F 28 A3
Sévérac-le-Château F 32 C1
Sevrier F 35 D4
Seyches F 31 D3
Seyne F 42 B4
Seyssel F 34 C4
Sézanne F 21 D4
Sheerness GB 4 A3
Shoeburyness GB 4 A3
Siddeburen NL 3 E3
Siegburg D 15 E4
Siegen D 15 F4
Sierck-les-Bains F 14 C1
Sierentz F 29 E4
Sierre CH 29 E1
Sigean F 39 E2
Signy-l'Abbaye F 13 F2
Sillé-le-Guillaume F 18 C4
Simmerath D 14 C4
Simmern D 15 E2
Simplon Dorf CH 29 F1
Singen D 23 F1
Sinzig D 15 E3
Sion CH 29 E1
Siorac-en-Périgord F 31 F3
Sissach CH 23 F4
Sisteron F 41 F4

58

Sittard NL 6 C1
Sittingbourne GB 4 A3
Six-Fours-les-Plages F 41 E1
Sizun F 8 B2
Sliedrecht NL 6 B3
Sloten NL 2 C3
Sluis F 5 E2
Sluis NL 5 F3
Smilde NL 3 E3
Sneek NL 3 D3
Soest NL 6 C4
Soestdijk NL 2 C1
Sögel D 3 F2
Soignies B 13 E4
Soissons F 13 D2
Soldeu AND 38 C2
Solenzara F 43 b1
Solingen D 7 E1
Solliès-Pont F 41 F2
Solothurn CH 29 E3
Sombernon F 28 A4
Sommesous F 21 E4
Sommières F 40 B3
Sonceboz CH 29 E3
Sonsbeck D 7 D2
Sopeira E 38 A1
Sore F 30 C2
Sort E 38 B1
Sos del Rey Católico E 36 B2
Sospel F 42 C3
Sotta F 43 b1
Souesmes F 19 F1
Soufflenheim F 23 E3
Souillac F 32 A3
Souilly F 22 A4
Soulac-sur-Mer F 24 A2
Soulaines-Dhuys F 21 E3
Soultz F 23 D1
Soultz F 23 E3
Soumoulou F 37 E3
Souppes-sur-Loing F 20 B3
Sourdeval F 10 B2
Sousceyrac F 32 B3
Soustons F 30 A2
Southend-on-Sea GB 4 A3
Southminster GB 4 A4
Souvigny F 26 C2
Spa B 14 C3
Spaichingen D 23 F1
Spakenburg NL 2 C1
Speyer D 23 F4
Spiez CH 29 F2
Spijkenisse NL 6 A3
Spotorno I 43 E3
Stadskanaal NL 3 E3
Stadtkyll D 15 D3
Stadtlohn D 7 E3
Stainville F 21 F3
Stalden CH 29 F1
Staplehurst GB 4 A3
Stavelot B 14 C3
Stavenisse NL 5 F3
Staveren NL 2 C3
Stechelberg CH 29 F1
Steenbergen NL 6 A3
Steenvoorde F 4 C1
Steenwijk NL 3 D2
Steinfurt D 7 F3
Stellendam NL 5 F3
Stenay F 14 A2
Stiens NL 3 D4
Stolberg D 14 C4
Straelen D 7 D2
Strasbourg F 23 E3
Stromberg D 15 E2
Stühlingen D 23 F1
Sturry GB 4 A3
Süchteln D 7 D2
Sudbury GB 4 A4
Suippes F 13 E1
Sully-sur-Loire F 20 A2
Sulz D 23 F2
Sumiswald CH 29 F2
Sundern D 7 F1

Surgères F 24 B3
Sursee CH 29 F3
Survilliers F 12 B1
Susa I 35 E2
Swalmen NL 6 C2
's Heerenberg NL 7 D3
's-Hertogen-Bosch NL 6 C3

T

Tafalla E 36 B2
Tain-l'Hermitage F 34 A2
Taizé F 27 F2
Tallard F 34 C1
Talloires F 35 D4
Talmont F 24 B2
Talmont-St-Hilaire F 24 A4
Tancarville F 11 E3
Taninges F 35 E4
Tarare F 34 A4
Tarascon F 40 C3
Tarascon-sur-Ariège F 38 C2
Tarbes F 37 E3
Tardets-Sorholus F 36 C3
Tarnos F 36 C4
Tartas F 30 B2
Taunusstein D 15 F2
Tauves F 32 C4
Tavannes CH 29 E3
Tavaux F 28 B3
Tavernes F 41 F2
Tecklenburg D 7 F3
Tegelen NL 7 D2
Telgte D 7 F3
Temse B 5 F2
Tence F 33 F3
Tende F 43 D3
Tenterden GB 4 A2
Ter Apel NL 3 F2
Terneuzen NL 5 F2
Terrasson-la-Villedieu F 31 F3
Tervuren B 6 A1
Tessy sur-Vire F 10 B2
Thalfang D 15 D2
Thann F 23 D1
Thaxted GB 4 A4
Thénezay F 25 D4
Thenon F 31 F4
Théoule F 42 B2
Thérouanne F 4 C1
Theux B 14 C4
Thiaucourt-Regniéville F 22 B4
Thiberville F 11 D2
Thiélbemont-Farémont F 21 E3
Thiers F 27 D1
Thionville F 14 C1
Thivars F 19 E4
Thiviers F 31 F4
Thizy F 27 E1
Thoissey F 27 F1
Tholey D 15 D1
Thonon F 28 C1
Thouarcé F 18 B2
Thouars F 18 B1
Thueyts F 33 F2
Thuir F 39 E1
Thun CH 29 E2
Thury-Harcourt F 10 C2
Tiel NL 6 C3
Tielt B 5 E2
Tienen B 6 B1
Tiercé F 18 B3
Tignes F 35 E3
Til-Châtel F 28 B4
Tilburg NL 6 B2
Tinchebray F 10 B2
Titisee D 23 E1
Titz D 7 D1
Todtmoos D 29 F4
Todtnau D 23 E1

Tongeren (Tongres) B 14 B4
Tongres (Tongeren) B 14 B4
Tonnay-Boutonne F 24 B2
Tonnay-Charente F 24 B2
Tonneins F 31 D2
Tonnerre F 21 D2
Torhout B 5 D2
Torigni-sur-Vire F 10 B2
Torino I 35 F2
Torla E 37 D1
Torre Pellice I 35 E1
Torriglia I 43 F4
Tôtes F 11 F3
Toucy F 20 C2
Toul F 22 B3
Toulon F 41 E2
Toulon-sur-Arroux F 27 E3
Tourcoing F 5 D1
Tournai (Doornik) B 13 D4
Tournan F 20 B4
Tournay F 37 E2
Tournon F 34 A2
Tournon-d'Agenais F 31 E2
Tournon-St-Martin F 25 E3
Tournus F 28 A2
Tours F 19 D2
Toury F 19 F3
Traben-Trarbach D 15 D2
Tramelan CH 29 E3
Trassem D 14 C1
Travers CH 29 D2
Trébeurden F 8 C3
Tréboul F 8 B2
Trégastel F 8 C3
Tréguier F 9 D2
Treignac F 32 B4
Treis D 15 E3
Tremp E 38 A1
Trets F 41 E2
Trévoux F 27 F1
Triaize F 24 A3
Triaucourt-en-
   Argonne F 21 F4
Triberg D 23 F2
Trie F 37 F3
Trier D 15 D2
Trittenheim D 15 D2
Troarn F 10 C2
Trois-Ponts B 14 C3
Trouville F 11 D3
Troyes F 21 D3
Truchtersheim F 23 E3
Trun F 11 D2
Tuchan F 39 E2
Tudela E 36 B1
Tuffé F 19 D3
Tulle F 32 B4
Tullins F 34 C3
Turckheim F 23 D2
Turnhout B 6 B2
Tuttlingen D 23 F1
Twist D 3 E2
Tzummarum NL 2 C3

U

Uckange F 14 C1
Uden NL 6 C3
Uelsen D 3 E2
Ugine F 35 D3
Uithoorn NL 2 B2
Uithuizen NL 3 E4
Ulmen D 15 D1
Unna D 7 F2
Urdos F 37 D2
Uriage-les-Bains F 34 C2
Urk NL 2 C2
Ury F 20 B3
Ussel F 32 C4
Ustaritz F 36 C3

Utrecht NL 6 B3
Uzel F 9 D1
Uzerche F 32 A4
Uzès F 40 C4

V

Vaas F 18 C2
Vaassen NL 3 D1
Vado Ligure I 43 E3
Vaiges F 18 B3
Vailly F 20 B1
Vailly F 13 D2
Vaison-la-Romaine F 41 D4
Val d'Esquières F 42 B2
Val d'Isère F 35 E3
Val Thorens F 35 D2
Val-Claret F 35 E3
Val-Suzon F 28 A4
Valberg F 42 B3
Valbonnais F 34 C2
Valcarlos E 36 C3
Valdahon F 28 C3
Valençay F 19 E1
Valence F 31 D1
Valence F 31 E2
Valence F 34 A2
Valence d'Albigeois F 32 B1
Valenciennes F 13 D4
Valensole F 41 F3
Valkenburg NL 6 C1
Valkenswaard NL 6 C2
Valleraugue F 40 B4
Vallet F 17 F2
Valloire F 35 D2
Vallon-en-Sully F 26 B3
Vallon-Pont-d'Arc F 33 F1
Vallorbe CH 28 C2
Vallorcine F 35 E4
Vallouise F 35 D2
Valmorel F 35 D3
Valognes F 10 B3
Valras-Plage F 39 F2
Valréas F 34 A1
Vals-les-Bains F 33 F2
Valtierra E 36 B1
Valtournenche I 35 F3
Vannes F 17 D3
Varades F 18 A2
Varazze I 43 E4
Varces F 34 C2
Varengeville-sur-Mer F 11 F3
Varennes-en-Argonne F 14 A1
Varennes-sur-Allier F 27 D2
Varilhes F 38 C3
Vars F 35 D1
Varsseveld NL 7 D3
Varzy F 27 D4
Vassy F 10 C2
Vatan F 26 A4
Vaucouleurs F 22 B3
Vauvert F 40 C3
Vauville F 10 A4
Vauvillers F 22 B1
Vayrac F 32 A3
Veendam NL 3 E3
Veenendaal NL 6 C3
Veere NL 5 E3
Veghel NL 6 C2
Velbert D 7 E2
Veldhoven D 6 C2
Velp NL 7 D3
Venaco F 43 b2
Vence F 42 C3
Vendargues F 40 B3
Vendeuvre F 21 E2
Vendôme F 19 D2
Venlo NL 7 D2
Venray NL 6 C2
Venta de Arraco E 36 C2

60

Ventimíglia I... 43 D3
Vera de Bidasoa E... 36 B3
Verberie F... 12 C2
Verbier CH... 35 F4
Verdun F... 22 A4
Verfeil F... 38 C4
Vergt F... 31 E3
Vermenton F... 20 C1
Vernet F... 38 C3
Vernet-les-Bains F... 39 D1
Verneuil F... 11 E1
Vernon F... 11 F2
Verny F... 22 C4
Verrès I... 35 F3
Verrières-de-Joux F... 29 D2
Versailles F... 12 B1
Versoix CH... 28 C1
Verteillac F... 24 C1
Vertus F... 21 D4
Verviers B... 14 C4
Vervins F... 13 E2
Verzuolo I... 35 F1
Verzy F... 13 E1
Vesoul F... 28 C4
Veules-les-Roses F... 11 E3
Veulettes-sur-Mer F... 11 E3
Veurne (Furnes) B... 5 D2
Vevey CH... 29 D1
Veynes F... 34 C1
Veyrier F... 35 D4
Vézelay F... 20 C1
Vézelise F... 22 B3
Vézénobres F... 40 C4
Viais F... 17 E2
Vianden L... 14 C2
Vianen NL... 6 B3
Vianne F... 31 D2
Vias F... 40 A3
Vibraye F... 19 D3
Vic F... 33 D4
Vic-en-Bigorre F... 37 E3
Vic-Fezensac F... 37 F4
Vic-sur-Aisne F... 12 C2
Vic-sur-Cère F... 32 C3
Vicdessos F... 38 B2
Vichy F... 27 D2
Vico F... 43 a2
Vidauban F... 42 A2
Viella E... 38 A2
Vielsalm B... 14 C3
Vienne F... 34 B3
Viersen D... 7 D2
Vierzon F... 19 F1
Vieux-Boucau-les-Bains F... 30 A2
Vif F... 34 C2
Vigneulles F... 22 B4
Vignory F... 21 F2
Vihiers F... 18 B2
Villaines-la-Juhel F... 18 C4
Villandraut F... 30 C3
Villandry F... 18 C2
Villard-de-Lans F... 34 C2
Villars F... 42 C3
Villars CH... 29 D1
Villars-les-Dombes F... 28 A1
Villé F... 23 D2
Ville-en-Tardenois F... 13 D1
Villebois-Lavalette F... 24 C1
Villedieu-les-Poêles F... 10 B2
Villefagnan F... 24 C2
Villefort F... 33 E1
Villefranche F... 42 C2
Villefranche-d'Albigeois F... 39 D4
Villefranche-de-Lauragais F... 38 C4
Villefranche-de-Lonchat F... 31 D4
Villefranche-de-Rouergue F... 32 B2
Villefranche-du-Périgord F... 31 E3
Villefranche-sur-Cher F... 19 E1
Villefranche-sur-Saône F... 27 F1
Villemur F... 31 F1
Villenauxe-la-Grande F... 21 D3

Villeneuve F... 32 B2
Villeneuve F... 41 D4
Villeneuve-de-Berg F... 33 F1
Villeneuve-de-Marsan F... 30 C2
Villeneuve-l'Archevêque F... 20 C3
Villeneuve-Loubet F... 42 C2
Villeneuve-sur-Allier F... 27 D3
Villeneuve-sur-Lot F... 31 E2
Villeneuve-sur-Yonne F... 20 C2
Villeréal F... 31 E3
Villers F... 11 D3
Villers-Bocage F... 10 C2
Villers-Bretonneux F... 12 C3
Villers-Cotterêts F... 12 C1
Villers-le-Lac F... 29 D3
Villers-St-Georges F... 20 C4
Villersexel F... 29 D4
Villerville F... 11 D3
Villingen D... 23 F1
Vimoutiers F... 11 D2
Vinádio I... 42 C4
Vinay F... 34 B3
Vinça F... 39 D1
Vinon-sur-Verdon F... 41 E3
Vire F... 10 B2
Vireux F... 34 C3
Virieu F... 34 C4
Virieu-le-Grand F... 34 C4
Virton B... 14 B2
Visé B... 14 C4
Visp CH... 29 F1
Vitré F... 18 A4
Vitry-le-François F... 21 E3
Vitteaux F... 27 F4
Vittel F... 22 B2
Vivario F... 43 b2
Viviers F... 34 A1
Vivonne F... 25 D3
Vizille F... 34 C2
Vizzavona F... 43 b2
Vlaardingen NL... 6 A3
Vlagtweed NL... 3 F3
Vlissingen NL... 5 E2
Void F... 22 B3
Voiron F... 34 C3
Voise F... 19 F4
Voix F... 41 E3
Volendam NL... 2 C2
Völklingen D... 23 D4
Voltri I... 43 F4
Voorschoten NL... 2 A1
Voorst NL... 7 D3
Voreppe F... 34 C3
Vorey F... 33 E3
Vouillé F... 25 D4
Vouvray F... 19 D2
Vouziers F... 13 F1
Voves F... 19 F3
Vreden D... 7 E3
Vresse B... 14 A2
Vron F... 12 B4
Vroomshoop NL... 3 E2
Vught NL... 6 B3

W

Waalwijk NL... 6 B3
Wageningen NL... 6 C3
Waldbröl D... 15 F4
Waldfischbach D... 23 E4
Waldkirch D... 23 E2
Walton-on-the-Naze GB... 4 B4
Waltrop D... 7 F2
Wangenbourg F... 23 D3
Waregem B... 5 E1
Waremme B... 14 B4
Warnsveld NL... 7 D3
Wasselonne F... 23 D3
Wassenaar NL... 2 A1
Wassenberg D... 7 D1

Wasserbillig L... 14 C2
Wassy F... 21 F3
Waterloo B... 13 F4
Waulsort B... 14 A3
Wavre B... 14 A4
Waxweiler D... 14 C3
Weener D... 3 F3
Weert NL... 6 C2
Weeze D... 7 D2
Wegberg D... 7 D1
Wehr D... 29 F4
Wehr D... 15 E3
Weilburg D... 15 F3
Well NL... 7 D2
Wellin B... 14 A3
Wemperhaardt L... 14 C3
Wengen CH... 29 F1
Wépion B... 14 A3
Werbomont B... 14 B3
Werdohl D... 7 F1
Werl D... 7 F2
Werlte D... 3 F2
Wermelskirchen D... 7 E1
Werne D... 7 F2
Wesel D... 7 D2
West Mersea GB... 4 A4
West-Terschelling NL... 2 C4
Westende-Bad B... 5 D2
Westerholt D... 3 F4
Westerlo B... 6 B1
Westkapelle NL... 5 E3
Wetter D... 7 F2
Wetteren B... 5 E1
Wettringen D... 7 F3
Whitstable GB... 4 A3
Wierden NL... 3 E2
Wiesbaden D... 15 F2
Wijhe NL... 3 D2
Wildbad D... 23 F3
Wildenrath D... 7 D1
Willebroek B... 6 A2
Willemstad NL... 6 A3
Willisau CH... 29 F3
Wilnsdorf D... 15 F4
Wiltz L... 14 C2
Wimereux F... 4 B2
Windeck D... 15 F4
Winnweiler D... 15 F1
Winschoten NL... 3 F3
Winsum NL... 3 E4
Winterswijk NL... 7 E3
Wipperfürth D... 7 E1
Wissant F... 4 B2
Wissembourg F... 23 E3
Wissen D... 15 F4
Witham GB... 4 A4
Witten D... 7 E2
Wittlich D... 15 D2
Woerden NL... 6 B4
Woerth F... 23 E3
Wolfach D... 23 F2
Wolfstein D... 15 E1
Wolhusen CH... 29 F2
Wolvega NL... 3 D3
Woodbridge GB... 4 B4
Worb CH... 29 E2
Workum NL... 2 C3
Wormerveer NL... 2 B2
Wormhout F... 4 C2
Worms D... 15 F1
Wörrstadt D... 15 F2
Wörth D... 23 F3
Wulfen D... 7 E2
Wuppertal D... 7 E1
Wuustwezel B... 6 A2

X

Xanten D... 7 D2
Xertigny F... 22 C2

Xhoffraix B... 14 C3

Y

Yenne F... 34 C3
Yerville F... 11 E3
Yesa E... 36 C2
Yport F... 11 E3
Ypres (Ieper) B... 5 D1
Yssingeaux F... 33 F3
Yverdon-les-Bains CH... 29 D2
Yvetot F... 11 E3
Yvoir B... 14 A3
Yvoire F... 28 C1

Z

Zaandam NL... 2 B2
Zaltbommel NL... 6 B3
Zandvoort NL... 2 B2
Zarautz E... 36 A3
Zeebrugge B... 5 E2
Zeist NL... 6 C3
Zell D... 15 E2
Zell D... 29 F4
Zelzate B... 5 E2
Zerf D... 15 D1
Zevenaar NL... 7 D3
Zevenbergen NL... 6 A3
Zicavo F... 43 b2
Zierikzee NL... 5 F3
Zijpe NL... 5 F3
Zinal CH... 29 E1
Zoetermeer NL... 6 B4
Zofingen CH... 29 F3
Zolder B... 6 B1
Zonza F... 43 b1
Zoutkamp NL... 3 E4
Zubiri E... 36 B3
Zuidhorn NL... 3 E3
Zuidlaren NL... 3 E3
Zülpich D... 15 D4
Zumaia E... 36 A4
Zundert NL... 6 B2
Zutphen NL... 7 D3
Zweibrücken D... 23 D4
Zweisimmen CH... 29 E2
Zwijndrecht NL... 6 B3
Zwolle NL... 3 D2